Going Gentle

A Guide to a Better Terminal Illness

Philip Graham

Grosvenor House
Publishing Limited

This book is published by
Grosvenor House Publishing Ltd
Link House
140 The Broadway, Tolworth, Surrey, KT6 7HT.
www.grosvenorhousepublishing.co.uk

A CIP record for this book
is available from the British Library

ISBN 978-1-80381-671-5

Table of contents

CHAPTER 1

Introduction

Over recent years, twenty-four of my good, long-standing friends have died. Two went suddenly and unexpectedly but all the others died after an illness lasting several months or, in a few cases, several years. Six of them had moderate or advanced dementia in the last few months or years of life. The final few hours and indeed days of most of them were usually but not always relatively smooth as life passed to a natural end. Many gradually became drowsy and died painlessly without any last agonising hours. A small number suffered dreadfully in the hours and days immediately before they died. In addition, during the months or years of their last illnesses many of them suffered serious, often extreme physical distress. Naturally, this was emotionally upsetting both to themselves and to their family members and friends. They may have had good deaths, but they certainly did not have good terminal illnesses. The fact that so many of my friends have died might seem surprising but will be less so when I reveal I'm over ninety and my late friends were nearly all in their eighties. In fact, all of the small number of long-standing friends I had from school and university as well as all my work colleagues who became close friends, have died. It has been a hard, deeply upsetting time.

Like everybody, though perhaps at a more conscious level than most, I have always had an interest in dying and death. In my forties, I became a member of the Voluntary Euthanasia Society. For nine years I was a Trustee, and for one year, Chair of its successor, Dignity in Dying, the organisation that campaigns for mentally competent people suffering from terminal illness to have the right to health care professional assistance if they have six months or less to go and wish to end their lives. For the past ten years I have edited the obituaries of prominent psychiatrists that are published in the Royal College of Psychiatrists journal, the *BJPsych Bulletin*. I also write obituaries. Indeed, I wrote obituaries that were published in *The Times*, *The Guardian* or elsewhere for seven of my late friends. It is to the obituaries I turn first when I open my daily newspaper. It is these that often seem to me to contain the only new 'news' in the paper. They often give amazing insights into the extraordinary lives of people of whom I had never previously heard.

Nobody finds it easy to think about, let alone even talk about dying and death. For some, it is a completely taboo subject. Avoidance of the subject staves off the natural anxiety associated with the topic. But, as one's own death or the death of a loved one approaches, this reticence needs to be overcome if one is going to have meaningful conversations about the future. Chapter 2,

'Thinking about dying and death', begins with an expression of opposition to the spirit of Dylan Thomas's poem 'Do not got gentle into that good night.' From what I have learned from the last illnesses of my friends, at this phase of life, it is far better both for oneself and for the members of one's family to be accepting of one's fate once it is clear that one is shortly going to die. 'Going gentle', if this is possible and sometimes for various reasons it is not, is the best way to go. I go on to discuss a number of questions which people nearing death and those close to them might ask themselves, hoping this will make it easier for such conversations to take place. Chapter 3 begins with a description of our bodily organs and goes on to describe how they are attacked by terminal conditions. I describe the course of the most common fatal illnesses. Some understanding of the pathology of the diseases that end our lives helps us to come to grips with what is happening to our bodies as they decline. Most even highly educated people have very little idea of the way their bodies function or how they gradually fail so I make no apology for including this strongly medical chapter. Chapter 4 provides a short account of the helping services, provided by the NHS and local authorities. The structure of these services is complicated and I hope this chapter will be a useful guide to how they function and who works in them.

In preparation for this book, I interviewed one or two surviving members of the family of each of my friends who had died. Usually this was the surviving partner or a child (now usually aged in their fifties) but in one case it was a niece. I describe this interview in chapter 5 and then go on in the following three chapters, beginning with chapter 6 to consider what I learned from the interview in terms of how the quality of life over the last few months or years of the person who had died might have been improved. Because this situation produces such special problems, chapter 7 describes what I learned about how one might improve quality of life when the terminally ill person has moderately severe or advanced dementia. Chapter 8 deals with the degree to which our friends had control over the timing of their deaths. This leads to a discussion of the implications of what I learned for proposed legalisation of assisted dying.

Chapter 9 deals with practical issues, some legal such as the thought that needs to go into making a will and how to prepare an advance decision and power of attorney. Some more personal issues are also discussed, such as sizing down if one is living in accommodation too large for one's needs and how to rid oneself of all the correspondence, papers and books that one has accumulated over the years and does not wish one's heirs to have to deal with. Chapter 10 discusses what we pass on to our successors after we die. Bearing in mind that for people without religious belief, such as myself and nearly all my late friends, it is what we leave behind of ourselves in *this* world that matters. So, this chapter inicludes a discussion of how we might, in our lifetimes, manufacture our main legacy, the memories of ourselves that others hold in their minds after we have gone. Chapter 11 briefly summarises how one can give oneself or a loved one who is dying the best chance of an easeful demise.

All but three of our late friends lived in London. Two lived in Paris and one in Berlin. Therefore, the contents of this book relate largely to the UK with health care provided by the NHS. It will however be relevant to those suffering from terminal illness in other countries. It will be obvious from my descriptions of them that my late friends were drawn from a privileged section of society. Just over half of them had an obituary published in a national newspaper after their death. They were all comfortably off and lived in relatively spacious accommodation. Death has been described as 'the great leveller.' There is one paramount respect in which this is indubitably true. When the rich are dead, they are just as dead as the poor. But income inequalities affect mortality just as they do every other part of life. People in lower social classes live much less long than do the wealthy. In London, men living in deprived areas of the city live seven years less than those in more affluent areas, only three or four miles away. The gap is even greater when it comes to the number of years spent in good health. Further, working class people are less likely to be able to access palliative care in hospices than are those in the middle classes. However, in other ways, social class differences are less important than one might expect. The evidence suggests that terminally ill working-class people get equal access to health care services compared to those in the middle classes. Further, perhaps because they are more geographically mobile, people in higher social classes actually have less family support during their terminal illnesses than do those in the working class. In fact, I suspect that what I write will be significantly relevant to all those who face a common end. Readers should remind themselves that if the last illnesses of the relatively affluent are as difficult as I describe, how much more so would this have been the case if my friends had had to cope with poverty, overcrowding and poor health care?

The fact that I have witnessed the final months and years of so many of my contemporaries made me think that, while I still have my cognitive faculties, I could write a book about dying and death that would be interesting and just possibly even helpful to those who wish to think more about their own deaths and the deaths of others. The book will therefore, I expect, be of most interest to those in their sixties and over but it could also be found valuable by younger people with older relatives in the last phase of life. Over the past few years, there have been a number of books written on this subject. Most have been written by physicians who have drawn on their clinical experience with people who have been their patients. Although a doctor myself, I have largely drawn on my experience not as a doctor, but as a friend, not only of the person who has died but of the surviving members of their families. Further, not surprisingly, with one or two notable exceptions such as Atul Gawande's *Being Mortal*, most of the physicians who have written about the end of life, have been palliative care physicians. Palliative care medicine developed from the admirable hospice movement founded by Dame Cicely Saunders, a British doctor with strong Christian beliefs. Although palliative care physicians are now much less likely to share her Christian beliefs, there remains a religious element to the movement. This puts emphasis on the sacred nature of human life. For this and doubtless other reasons, physicians working in palliative care have been more opposed than other doctors to changes in the law which would allow people who are mentally competent and terminally ill to have professional healthcare assistance to end their lives when they see them as having no value. An alternative perspective is that the value of a human life does not depend on the existence of a divine presence and can only be judged by the person who is living it. This is a crucial distinction, particularly when life is most at risk, - namely at its very end. This book therefore, although respectful to those with religious beliefs, largely provides a non-religious perspective on death and dying shared by many others in the general population.

For understandable reasons, some of the family members of my late friends did not wish their names to appear in the book. I have therefore anonymised all references to individuals except where I am quoting their published work or information about them that is available in the public domain.

CHAPTER 2

Thinking about dying and death

Facing Death: A Personal Account

As Dylan Thomas's father neared death, the poet wrote one of his best-known poems. In it he encouraged his father to fight hard against his terminal illness, postponing his inevitable fate for as long as possible.

> Do not go gentle into that good night.
> Old age should burn and rave at close of day
> Rage, rage, against the dying of the light.

Having listened to the accounts of the final weeks, months and even years of my late friends and read the wise advice given by many palliative care doctors and nurses, my conclusion is that, brilliant though the poem is, it conveys an extremely unhelpful message. It is true that, in the early stages of a terminal illness, when the outcome is in doubt, an optimistic frame of mind and a determination to survive and live life to the full for as long as possible are highly desirable. Remaining as active as one's symptoms allow should not be seen as a denial of death but as a sign that one is making the most of what is left of one's life. But there comes a point when one has to say 'enough is enough'. At this point, the aim should be to go as gentle as possible.

Those who write about terminal illness often use military language. One is encouraged to 'fight' one's illness. If the illness is cancer, then one is seen as engaged in a 'battle against cancer', a 'conflict' literally to the death. But the good soldier knows when to surrender, when prolonging a struggle merely extends the length of time spent in pointless suffering. Once it becomes clear that death is inevitable and soon on its way, exactly the opposite message to the one given in the poem is needed. Struggling against the inevitable increases the distress of the ill person as well as members of the family and makes medical and nursing care harder.

My own experience

I would not be writing this book if I had experienced the entire journey from terminal diagnosis to death as all the twenty-four friends I have lost have done. The nearest I can come to a personal account of facing death arises from an unexpected illness I experienced in my sixtieth year. My wife and I were on a train to a small town in Switzerland to enjoy a ski walking holiday when I suddenly noticed I was bleeding bright red blood from my 'back passage'. We rejected the idea of going straight back to Zurich where we had boarded the train. This was foolish as the medical facilities would have been much better there. Anyway, we arrived at our hotel in the skiing village where the bleeding continued.

A doctor was called, and I was rapidly admitted to the local hospital, more used to dealing with broken bones. After wrongly pursuing, for a day or two, the idea that the bleeding might have come as a result of my taking a couple of non-steroid anti-inflammatory tablets, a surgeon was called. He was unable to make a diagnosis so he opened up my abdomen to find out what might be the cause of the problem. It turned out that I had suffered an intussusception, a folding in of the lower part of my intestine. This was causing an obstruction to the passage of faeces and a rupture to a small artery which was bleeding into my gut. It is a condition usually occurring in infancy. When it happens, as it rarely does, in adulthood, it usually means there is some serious condition present such as a cancer.

The surgeon unfolded my intestine, straightened it up, noted there did not seem to be any other pathology and sewed me up again. He and I expected this would have resolved the problem. Unfortunately, after a couple of days, I had a recurrence of quite severe pain in my abdomen. It was at this point that the surgeon went away for a couple of days to attend a conference in Zurich. He was the only general surgeon in the hospital, and I was left in pain and in a highly anxious state. When he returned, I told him I had dreamed about him. In his Swiss-German which I was just about able to understand, he told me he had also dreamed about me. This was not a trivial event in my life or, so it turned out, in his.

There was nothing for it, he had to open me up again. The intussusception had recurred. He repeated the procedure he had carried out previously, but this time he inserted a very long tube from my mouth right down to beyond the obstruction to prevent any further recurrence. There the surgery ended but the doctors who looked after me were clearly not very experienced in managing the fluid balance of a post-operative patient. I became breathless. It was at this point that my daughter, a relatively newly qualified doctor, arrived from London. She had recently completed her house jobs in medicine and surgery. After talking to the Swiss doctors, she went through my charts and decided I needed to be transferred to a London hospital. I was suffering from pulmonary oedema, a potentially fatal condition in which the lungs are overloaded with fluids.

By a great stroke of luck, I had taken out health insurance in Heathrow Terminal Two on my outward journey. In fact, I had had in mind the possibility of a skiing accident but, of course, the insurance covered all health eventualities. So, expense was not a problem. Within twenty-four hours, Anna, my daughter, had arranged for me to be admitted to the Whittington Hospital, less than half a mile from my home in London, and I was in a tiny ambulance plane on my way back home. The crew had picked up sandwiches in England from Marks and Spencer on their way to the plane and, while I looked on from behind my oxygen mask, my wife and the accompanying nurse munched away. The ward in the hospital in Switzerland had been immaculate with gleaming hospital furniture. The Whittington ward was in a poor state of decorative repair, but the doctors were highly skilled in post-operative care. Within a week, my fluid balance had been put right and the tube removed. Within about six weeks, I was back at work.

During my illness, which admittedly only lasted around a month, I had had to face the possibility I might die. Without an operation, indeed without the two operations, I certainly would have died. I might also have died from post-operative complications. As a doctor, I was well aware of these possibilities and that my life might end at that point. Looking back today, just over thirty years later, I have tried to reconstruct the thoughts and feelings I experienced at the time.

A good deal of the time while I was lying ill in my hospital bed, I was in no fit state to reflect on my fate. For many days, I had pretty severe intermittent pain in my belly which interfered with any other thoughts. Later, I was too breathless to think about much else. When I was able to think about other matters, I was taken up with wondering whether my affairs were in good order, whether my will was up to date, whether I had left any papers in my desk that I would prefer not to come to light after my death and so on. Fortunately, I was able to conclude that I did not have too much to worry about on these scores. I was therefore left, in my relatively symptom-free moments, to ask myself a series of questions and to ponder on possible answers.

For many people, though by no means all, entering the final phase of life triggers questioning about the fundamentals of existence. For some of us, and this was certainly the case as far as I was concerned, 'going gentle' depended, at least to some extent, on my having reflected on these questions. I came to few definite conclusions but felt calmer for having tried. Perhaps others may feel the same. I hope what follows may be helpful as a starting point to those who ask themselves the same or similar questions. I make no apology for the fact that these questions are not arranged in any coherent order. A certain wandering of thought is surely permissible when one thinks one may be at or near the end of one's life. In fact, I wasn't at the end of my life, but I didn't know that at the time.

Question 1. Why do we need to die?

I find the most convincing reason lies in evolutionary theory. This explains why, for the survival of the human species, our bodies have built-in obsolescence; we must all die. As the environment changes, we need to develop new genes to ensure we can meet new circumstances. These arise as a result of gene mutations, - random variations of the existing gene structure, the most effectively adaptive of which are passed on to our children. To make space for these new, better-equipped people, the existing population must die off. Explanations (that I shall discuss later in some detail) involving a deity who has given our lives a universal meaning and has prepared a better life for us after death are therefore unnecessary though they are of deep significance to many people. We must die so that the species can live on.

Let me suggest a thought experiment. If, in some brave new world, scientists, by genetic manipulation, created a race of human beings immune to disease who lived to a hundred with all their faculties intact. This new species might decide that a hundred years was long enough for a life span and arrange for an assisted death at this age in order to make room for the next generation with slightly improved genes. When, as they approached death, they considered the meaning of their lives, the members of this species would surely, like today's non-believers, find it in their families, their friendships and the way they had spent their time on earth. They would know that they had not been created in order to fulfil some divine purpose but had emerged as a result of genetic engineering. We, the people of today, are in a similar situation. The only difference is that the new species would know its existence depended on active genetic manipulation; we have good reason to think that our continued existence arises by chance alone. There is no reason why the absence of any universal meaning should trouble us any more than it would distress the members of our new species because they were suffering or remembering what it was like to be alive.

Question 2. How do my religious beliefs fit with those in the general population?

At the end of their lives, people are inevitably drawn to think of their attitudes to religion. This certainly happened to me when I was very ill in Switzerland. I first found myself asking myself about my own religious beliefs and how they compared with those of others. I first found myself making a distinction between belonging to a particular religion and having beliefs about the existence of a personal God and the likelihood of there being some sort of afterlife after death. For many people, (probably the majority if one takes the global population), these two coincide, - what the religion they belong to teaches and what they believe are identical. These fundamentalists, who may be Christian, Jewish or Muslim, believe in the literal truth of the holy books of their particular religion. They have a clear idea of the way their conduct during life will determine what happens to them in their afterlife. This may be comforting or anxiety-provoking. Further, they are 'sustained' by their faith which gives their life, including their suffering, an important meaning.

There are also many people who may or may not belong to one or other of the organised religions who have religious ideas that are more complicated and perhaps more tentatively held. These people may, for example, believe that our material reality is not the only reality, indeed that there is a more fundamental form of existence that is mysterious and unknowable to us using the reason and logic with which we address difficult questions about the material world. Such people are unlikely to believe in the literal truth of the holy scripts but think that, all the same, they contain much wisdom. During their terminal illnesses, they may find their faith in another reality both sustaining and helpful, giving meaning to their lives, even though they are likely to be sceptical of any sort of afterlife.

What is certain is that whatever the nature of our religious beliefs, we are far from alone. While the prevalence of religious belief in the general population in the western world and, in particular in Britain, is, as we shall see, declining, there are still very large numbers of people who turn to religion when they search for meaning in their lives. While there is vast variability in the religious beliefs of the general population, findings from the 2021 National Census suggest that the British population is rather rapidly becoming increasingly less likely to regard itself as Christian and increasingly more likely to see itself as having 'no religion'. For the first time since Census data were collected in 1801, in answer to the question as to which religion you belong to, less than half the British population (46.2%) described themselves as Christian, a decline of 13.1% from the figure found only ten years earlier in 2011. 'No religion' was the second commonest response at 37.2% up from 25.2% ten years earlier.

But the fact that people say they have 'no religion' does not necessarily mean they do not believe in God. A report from Theos, a think tank exploring religious matters on the beliefs of those who tick 'none of the above' when asked in the National Census which religion they belong to (the so-called Nones), produced some surprising findings in this respect. The survey found that that only about half (51%) of the Nones, (those who identified themselves as not belonging to any religion) said they did not believe in God, and a fifth (20%) said they definitely or probably believed in life after death. There were three, broadly equal-sized clusters of people among the nones. Those the survey identified as 'campaigning' nones were hostile to religion and regarded it as their mission to persuade others to become 'nones', The second cluster, so-called 'spiritual nones', were less fervently atheistic and more open to the importance of spiritual experiences. A third cluster, 'tolerant nones', among whom I would count myself, were atheist in their beliefs, but more accepting of the fact that many people did subscribe to particular religious beliefs than those in the first group.

Question 3. What types of non-belief are there?

People who have religious beliefs see life as having a universal meaning given to it by a divine presence. Among those without religious beliefs, there is a distinction between those, often calling themselves humanists, who see life as having a universal meaning and those who do not. The universal meaning that humanists identify is derived from their belief that our values and ethical decisions emerge not from some higher authority but from the reason, empathy and concern for others that are characteristic of human beings. They see humanity as engaged in a search for moral progress, moving towards a higher form of existence with each generation.

In his seven-fold classification of atheism, John Gray described this particular pattern of belief as less distinct from religion than perhaps humanists like to think. He calls it 'secular humanism' and sees it as a form of religion that is only apparently different from the religions of the past. Humanists have replaced God with humanity, with science and scientific findings as the humanist Bible and scientists as its new priests. Some humanists claim the high moral ground, attributing their beliefs to unanswerable scientific findings emerging, for example, from the study of evolution. But, as Gray points out, science is a method and cannot claim to state truths. For him, humanists are believers just like Christians, Jews and Muslims are believers; they merely have faith in different ideas. In contrast, some people without religion such as myself who are not humanists see life as essentially without any form of *universal* meaning. Nevertheless, we all endow life with a *personal* meaning derived from our upbringing and from the values of the society in which we live. Everyone gives life their own personal meaning which has great significance for them.

Question 4. What has been my own religious pathway?

People at the end of their lives are inevitably drawn to think of their own attitudes to religion and the way this developed. This certainly happened to me when I was very ill in Switzerland. Let me begin therefore with an account of my own religious pathway. I have done this at some length as I imagine many others who are very seriously ill may wish to spend considerable time reflecting on the pathway they have taken to their own religious beliefs or, more commonly, lack of them.

I was brought up as an orthodox, though not an ultra-orthodox Jew. My father was born in Konigsberg, now Kaliningrad, in what is now part of Russia but was then in Prussia, in eastern Germany. As a boy, he sang in the synagogue choir. In 1907, when he was 22, having trained to be a dentist, he emigrated to England and, in 1931, had a marriage arranged through his synagogue with my mother, who was also Jewish though less orthodox. He was, an active member of synagogues in Luton and Dunstable, in Bedfordshire, and then in central London. He always attended services on (Sabbath) Saturday mornings. We observed the religious festivals as well as the dietary laws but otherwise lived a life very similar to our neighbours.

At birth, I was brought up in this orthodox Jewish household. At the age of ten, I was sent away to a Jewish boarding house, part of a direct grant, now an independent school in Cambridge. Here there were Jewish prayers morning and evening, and we did not go to school, as others did, on Saturday mornings. Instead, we walked to the synagogue on the other side of the city to attend a religious service. At thirteen, I had a barmitzvah and to begin with continued to say morning and evening prayers. However, a year after my barmitzvah, at fourteen, I started to think that it was foolish to observe the Sabbath or to follow dietary and other Jewish laws when these had been laid down millennia ago and seemed no longer relevant. I told my father this news. This was 1946. Much that had been hidden about the Holocaust had now emerged. Indeed, the sermon at my barmitzvah in September 1945 was given by an Army chaplain who had visited Belsen shortly after its liberation. If God was omniscient, how could he not have known about it? If omnipotent, why did He not stop it? My father suggested I wrote expressing my misgivings to the minister at the synagogue in London we were then attending. He would put me right. I did so, and the minister wrote back explaining why I should follow the rules laid down by my religion. I found his arguments unconvincing and after a further exchange of letters with a similar outcome, my father accepted that I would no longer obey the Jewish laws. Since that time, I have regarded myself as a secular Jew, neither attending religious services nor conforming to the rules laid down for Jews to follow. I lost the tenuous religious beliefs I had previously held but continued to have a Jewish identity.

So, my first rejection of religion was almost entirely related to Jewish rituals and practices. This was not coincidental. The emphasis in Judaism at least at the time I was growing up, was on keeping to the laws as stated in the five books of Moses. I was expected to believe in a divine Creator and to behave morally as laid down in the Ten Commandments, but such belief and moral behaviour were not seen as central to my religious identity. Eating food like shellfish or pork, as I maybe mistakenly understood it, was at least if not more sinful than telling a lie or stealing.

As I grew into adulthood, my rejection of rituals and practice extended to include a rejection of all the other ideas that come with adherence to a particular religion - the existence of a divine Creator, of a divinely inspired moral order and of an afterlife. Increasingly, I saw the world as having no universal meaning. Nevertheless, my own life had a personal meaning derived from my upbringing and the society in which I lived. All this did not mean I lost my identity as a Jew, albeit a secular Jew. However, for many years, being Jewish hardly ever crossed my mind. Further, occasional conversations made me think that my Jewishness hardly crossed the minds of others; rarely was I seen socially as Jewish. Very occasionally, if it looked as though someone was about to tell an antisemitic joke, I declared my Jewish origins to save the speaker embarrassment.

On two occasions I took part in demonstrations in London relating to the State of Israel. In October 1973, when it was wrongly believed that Israel was in danger of total destruction at the beginning of the Yom Kippur War, I attended a rally to support Israel and to demand the British government provide support for it. As it turned out, Israel had no need of support from the British government. Many years later, on Sunday, 11 January 2009, I stood in Trafalgar Square with a small group of Jews strongly opposed to aggressive Israeli government policies towards the Palestinians. We were cordoned off for our protection, while a large procession of Israel-supportive Jews marched past us in support of those policies. As they passed by and realised who we were, this procession of Israel-supportive Jews swore and spat at us. It was a new experience for me, reserved until my seventy-eighth year, to be spat at. I felt very Jewish.

Then, when Jeremy Corbyn became Leader of the Labour Party in 2015 and it was alleged there was much antisemitism in the political party to which I belonged, I began to think of myself as a secular Jew on a daily basis. In the frequent discussion there was about the matter, I always declared my Jewish origins. It was a strange arousal of Jewish identity which largely ceased when Corbyn lost the leadership in 2019.

My atheist beliefs

My rejection of the idea of universal meaning largely arose because of increasing awareness of the immensity of the universe and the minuscule amount of space taken up by our own planet. The discoveries made by astrophysicists have made it impossible for me to believe that there is any universal meaning or significance in our lives.

Life as a frozen pea

Almost exactly a hundred years ago, a young American astronomer, Edwin Hubble, began to make observations which were to lead to the discovery of the mind-boggling immensity of the size of the whole universe. He took a photograph of a star which turned out to be 2.5 million light-years away. As everyone now knows, our planet is a minuscule component of a galaxy, a system of stars and gases, the Milky Way. This galaxy is only one of countless others. There are many billions of such galaxies out there. It has been estimated that if each galaxy was represented by a frozen pea, the number of frozen peas would fill the Albert Hall. Then, if one thinks of the miniscule volume one fills oneself in our own galaxy, there would be enough peas of similar size to fill the Albert Hall again. Surely the life of someone the size of a human being cannot have an existence that is meaningful in any cosmic or universal sense which it would have to be if we were objects of divine concern. Our understanding of the size of the universe means that, for me though of course not for many, many others, any idea of *universal* meaningfulness is laughable. This in no way indicates that the meanings we, as human beings, create for ourselves do not have enormous personal significance. Clearly, they do. Awareness of our infinitely tiny place in the universe need not diminish the way we see our lives as personally significant.

Life as stardust

I have found another story drawing on our place in the universe to be helpful in thinking about the nature of the material reality of our world. It was told by the eloquent and inspiring sociologist, Erik Olin Wright, who died in 2019. During his eleven-month terminal illness, he wrote a blog which was turned into a book, *Stardust to Stardust* in which he reflected on the ways a materialist like himself could not just explain but joyfully celebrate his own existence. The emergence of human consciousness after billions of years of the existence of the universe, Wright sees as almost but not quite miraculous, - not quite miraculous because, after all, he only believed in a fully material world in which miracles do not occur. His consciousness gave him what he saw as the immense privilege of the whole range of emotional and intellectual experiences he enjoyed throughout his life and continued to enjoy in his final months until the material of which his body was made, returned to the ecosystem. Inspirational though Wright's book is, it does not point to the existence of any kind of reality different from the material world of which we are all aware.

Life as a leaf

Another expression linking human life to the natural world was offered by Herbert Read, an art historian and literary critic, who happened to be the father of one of my friends who has recently died. He wrote:

> 'The death of each of us is in the order of things – it follows life as surely as night follows day. We can take the tree of life as a symbol. The human race is the trunk and the branches of the tree, and individual men and women the leaves, which appear for a season, flourish for a summer and then die.

> I too, am like a leaf of this tree, and one day I will be torn off by a storm, or simply decay and fall, and become part of the earth about its roots – but while I live, I am conscious of the tree's flowing sap and steadfast strength. Deep down in my

consciousness, is the consciousness of a collective life, a life of which I am a part and to which I make a minute but unique contribution.

When I die and fall, the tree remains, nourished to some degree by my manifestation of life. Millions of leaves have preceded me, and millions will follow me – but the tree itself grows and endures.'

Life as a throw of the dice

A series of discoveries of the importance of chance or contingency in the lives we lead has further strengthened my sense of the arbitrary nature of the lives we all lead. Again, let me use myself as an example. I was born in 1932 into a middle-class family in Luton, a medium-sized town thirty miles north of London. As a result of the place and year of my birth and my social class, I have been able to lead a life almost entirely free from significant social stress. Because of my year of birth, I have not had to fight in a world war. The second World War had little impact on my life as Luton was the target of very little bombing, and my father was too old to serve in the military. After a privileged education in a direct-grant school, bought at modest cost, my university education was free, and I then moved post World War 2 into a world of full employment. After an enjoyable, well-paid career, I retired with a public service pension sufficient to meet all my needs. Meanwhile Luton prospered, especially following the development of its airport, soon to become the fourth largest in the UK.

Let me contrast this life with that I would have led if I had been born (as I well might have been), in 1932 in Tangshan, a medium-sized town in northern China about the same distance from the capital city, Beijing as Luton is from London. I would first have had to live through the brutal Japanese invasion from 1937 to 1941 and then the Civil War between the Nationalists and the Communists from 1938 to 1949 when the People's Republic of China was established. It is highly likely that by 1949 my father would have been killed fighting on one side or the other and I would have been brought up by my mother. Then came the great famine of 1959-1961 in which, if I had survived thus far, I might well have starved. The Cultural Revolution lasting from 1966-1976 brought further social disruption, especially to middle-class families. If I had lived this long and had a professional job, I would have been sent out into the country to labour in the fields. In the unlikely event that my life continued, I would almost certainly have been killed in 1976, with 265,000 others, in the great earthquake that struck Tangshan which was at its epicentre. At every age, my chances of starvation or violent death would have been immeasurably greater in China than in England.

Scientific discoveries in the field of genetics have also revealed the equally important ways in which chance has played a fundamental role in my existence. When I was conceived, half my father's DNA was combined with half my mother's. The halves of their DNA which, by chance, I did not inherit would have made me an entirely different person. For example, if I had inherited my father's X chromosome rather than his Y and there was a 50% chance of that, I would have been a girl. But it is also certain that if I had inherited the other halves of my parents' genetic make-up, I would be different in physical appearance as well as in personality and in intelligence, both moderately heritable characteristics. It is not only in the development of personal characteristics that chance is important. When the genetic material of two parents combine at the moment of conception, slight variations or mutations may occur. If a mutation produces an offspring with improved survival prospects, that offspring will have an improved chance of passing on the mutation in turn to its progeny. It is in this way rather than by any divine intervention that species change and develop. Surely, if blind chance plays such a vital part in our development, there is very little point in looking for some sort of universal meaning in our lives. We exist as we do because of the hand we have been dealt in the game of life. If the cards had been shuffled differently, we would have been different too.

Question 5. What were the religious views of my late friends

All of my interviews with the family members of my friends who had died recently included a brief conversation about the religious views of the person who had died and, in particular, whether they believed in an afterlife. I shall discuss my friends' religious views as described in the interviews but will also refer to the views a small number of them had published during their lifetimes. An atheist was defined by one of my late friends, Mary Warnock, in her book *Dishonest to God* as 'one who recognises that some people believe something that he or she denies, namely that God exists.' She described herself as an 'Anglican atheist', by which she meant that, while she did not believe in God or an afterlife, she was deeply attached to the Anglican liturgy and loved much sacred music.

Some of my other friends did have a vague idea of the existence of a divine entity, but only two of my twenty-four close friends who have died over recent years (both of whom had strong Christian beliefs) believed in any sort of afterlife, and they, only tentatively. A small number expressed themselves in a way that suggested there was just a remote possibility of some existence after death. One, in his last days, expressed his awareness of his impending death by saying on more than one occasion, - 'If the good Lord wants to take me over the waterfall of life, so be it.' I visited this friend two days before he died. When I left him, I said that I hoped to see him again. He replied: 'I hope so too', but whereas I was expressing a hope I would see him alive in a few days, I know he was hoping to see me in another world. I was disappointed in my hope, and strongly suspect that he will never know his own wish was not fulfilled. Of my other friends, none had any firm belief in an afterlife and nearly all were firmly convinced there would be no such thing. One, a secular Jew, though moderately orthodox in following Jewish dietary laws, attending the synagogue on holy days and strongly identifying with the Jewish community, had no belief in an afterlife. Another, a practising Catholic, was encouraged by his Jesuit priest to believe in a heaven. The best he could muster in response to his priest was an agreement that he would 'wait and see'.

Most of the surviving family members I interviewed were also disbelieving. The widow of one of my late friends was expelled from her Sunday school at the age of twelve for having asked an awkward question: 'If Cain and Abel were the only children of Adam and Eve, how could any more children have been born?' She was told to leave and not come back. She has never wavered in her atheist beliefs which have, if anything, been confirmed by what she sees as inflexibility in those who belong to an organised religion. Another family member whose wife had died, who himself came to England to escape the Nazis in 1939 on a kinder-transport, asked me 'How could I possibly believe in God or an afterlife after the Holocaust?'

A number of our friends, while not believing in God or in an afterlife, and therefore atheists, identified themselves as humanists. Indeed, my friend, Jonathan Miller served for a time as President of the British Humanist Association (BHA), now the Humanists UK. Similarly, others were members of the BHA. Doubtless others either belonged to the BHA or held beliefs very close to humanism. In fact, only a tiny number of people who lack religious beliefs are members of Humanists UK (total membership 100,000) so our friends were atypical in this respect. One or two preferred to support the National Secular Society which does not profess any beliefs about the meaning of life and limits its aims to ensuring that people who do not subscribe to any religion suffer no disadvantages in public life. In contrast, Mary Warnock, said she did not want to be associated with any -ism.

My late friend, Michael Rutter, identified himself for much of his life as a Quaker. In his book *The Measure of Our Values*, in which he considered goals and values in the upbringing of children, he subscribed to the idea that the essence of Quakerism was the concept of 'That of God in everyone,' but noted that there was wide divergence in quite what 'God' meant in that context. 'At one extreme would be those who, in traditional Christian fashion, think of God in terms of a being – the creator and orderer of the universe, almighty and eternal. At the other, would be those who come much closer to the humanist tradition in their agnostic position on the notion of any divine intervention in the material world. For this latter group, in which I would place myself, the assumption of God as a creator is not capable of validation by experience and hence falls into the class of 'inessential assumptions'....'

My interviews with family members suggested that absence of religious belief was held on a spectrum of certainty. A friend at one end of the spectrum of atheism completely rejected the idea of a personal God and totally dismissed the idea of an afterlife. Another, while discounting the idea of an afterlife, probably entertained the possibility of some sort of divine presence. How else, he asked himself, could the universe have come into existence? It was his answer to the fundamental question – Why is there something rather than nothing? Commonly among my friends, there was mild inconsistency or variability over time in their religious beliefs. Her children thought this might have been true for Mary Warnock herself. None of my friends, as it happens, turned to religion at the end of their lives in the hope they might survive their physical death. But there were many who, during their lifetimes, wavered between firm atheism and agnosticism out of unwillingness to reject completely an implausible possibility. One friend, who had taken no interest in her own Jewishness from adolescence until the age of about eighty, suddenly became interested in various aspects of Judaism and read around them, but two or three years later, before she died, dropped all curiosity about the matter. Others took a committed agnostic position. One told me he thought agnosticism was the only respectable intellectual position and this was what he continued to think until he developed dementia and was unable to express any sort of opinion on the matter.

Various personality characteristics appeared to determine the position my friends took up on this matter. Those who were decisive and tolerated uncertainly with difficulty tended towards firm atheist belief. On the other hand, those with an optimistic personality were largely unwilling to discard the possibility of an afterlife no matter how remote that possibility might be. As I have said, there were only two or three committed Christians among my friends. Neither thought it at all likely there was any sort of afterlife. The more cautious and generally sceptical among my friends were unwilling to commit themselves to any set of beliefs on these fundamental matters. One friend did not believe in the existence of God but, for some reason possibly linked in his case to a strong sense of Jewishness, would not have wanted to be thought an atheist. Further, a number of my friends who did not believe in any sort of God did confide to members of their family that they would have liked to be a believer. Julian Barnes put this very clearly, when he began his book about death, *Nothing To Be Frightened Of*, 'I don't believe in God, but I miss him.'

Only a small number of my friends were what John Gray calls 'God-haters'. Perhaps the best-known God-hater is the evolutionary biologist, Richard Dawkins, the title of whose books *The God Delusion* and *Outgrowing God* do not convey the venom with which he expresses his detestation of the idea of a divine presence and of all religions. He points particularly to the conflicts between religions both in the past and currently that have been responsible for the suffering and deaths of millions of people. Of my late friends, probably only Jonathan Miller could be regarded as a God-hater, but this would not be a totally accurate description either. As his public pronouncements revealed, he was really a religion-hater who abhorred the idea of God as adopted by nearly all religions. Despite having a moderately observant Jewish father, he embraced atheism early on in his adolescence. Famously, in a sketch performed in the highly successful 1960s revue, *Beyond The Fringe*, he described himself as 'not really a Jew, just Jew-ish, not the whole hog, you know.' His BBC programmes on the history of atheism concluded with some reflections on his own mortality. He firmly believed in death meaning extinction and said he wasted no time in thinking about the idea that he might, after all, wake up somewhere else and be shown, red-faced, to have been a fool. God-haters, as I have described them, fall into the cluster characterised in the Theos survey described above as 'campaigning nones.' Jonathan Miller was against any kind of zealotry, for or against religion.

Similarly, most of our late friends who were atheists or agnostics were not God-haters. They acknowledged the terrible atrocities committed especially by religious fundamentalists, and one or two, at least, hated religions, but many also recognised, as I do myself, the tremendous amount of good work done in the world, carried out especially by charitable religious organisations. At an international level, many of the humanitarian charities are inspired by religious faith. Locally, churches, mosques and synagogues are often responsible for the most significant contributions to the welfare of disadvantaged people made at a community level. Whether the good carried out in the name of religion more than balances out the harm is a moot question – but it is important, as most of our atheist friends acknowledged, to recognise the good religions do as well as the evil.

It is noteworthy that my interviews with surviving family members also revealed that husbands and wives, with one or two exceptions, talked remarkably little to each other about the existence of God or the possibility of an afterlife. With many couples, this was because of an assumption that they had shared views and therefore there was nothing to talk about. With quite a few however, the surviving family member felt in more than a little doubt about what the person who had died did actually believe. Fear of death may have contributed to an unwillingness to discuss the matter. One widow of a late friend could not remember a time when she and her husband had discussed their own religious beliefs or belief in an afterlife. They were both signed up members of Humanists UK because they were impressed with the way the organisation's celebrants conducted the funerals they had attended. They were both turned against religion by the way the husband's orthodox Jewish parents had refused for many years to have anything to do with his non-Jewish wife. Despite the lack of any discussion of the subject, the widow was sure that her late husband was, as she remains, agnostic. In fact, most of my friends were singularly focussed on what they spent time thinking about and tended to avoid pondering on matters over which they felt they had little control.

Question 6. In the absence of religious belief, where does morality come from?

When, as part of my professional work, I wrote about moral development in children, I concluded that moral or 'good' behaviour emerges largely from our upbringing when our parents answer our questions about what is fair? Questions about fairness and unfairness are universal in childhood. They are asked especially frequently when children believe they have been unfairly treated. The most satisfactory answers given by parents reveal how difficult it is to judge fairness, how much it involves compromise, and how an attempt to lay down hard and fast principles whether or not by recourse to religious authority, leads to obvious unfairness. The conversations children have with their parents nevertheless lead to the way certain human qualities such as honesty, generosity, unselfishness and caring can and indeed should be regarded as good because they result in a sense of wellbeing in others and oneself, and other, equally human qualities, such as greed, selfishness, lying and stealing can and indeed should be regarded as bad or, in their extreme form, evil because they result in harm to others and oneself.

As children grow into teenage and then adulthood, their ideas about right and wrong are elaborated by their experiences at school, with teachers and then friends, and then finally in the adult world. The complexities of the society in which human beings live inevitably result in conflicts between different 'right' courses of action. It is not that human beings are, by their nature, imperfect, but that the structure of the societies which have evolved over time, has not allowed simple answers to ethical questions of right and wrong. This does not mean there are no answers; only that simple answers are unusual (though they certainly exist in some cases) and complicated answers are more often appropriate.

My own values largely developed in my childhood and adolescence and have remained the principles by which I have tried to lead my life ever since. So, I try to be honest, truthful, caring, generous, and hard-working. I hope to be judged by others according to the degree to which I adhere to these values.

My late friend, the philosopher Mary Warnock, put this point of view more eloquently than I can. She wrote: 'Has morality then, in reality, no more than human authority? I do not believe it has; but this does not entail that it must be completely uncertain or that there is no real difference between how we must and how we must not behave. For human beings alone among animals can envisage a world that is better than their own. They can understand the faults, the hazards and the horrors of their own even if it is others, not themselves, who suffer. They have much in common and can sympathize with each other. This is part of human nature though it needs to be taught. Morality arises as the predicament of human beings in the world is recognized and their shared responsibility for one another is understood.'

Question 7. How do non-believers account for spiritual experiences

When Jonathan Miller was making his series of BBC programmes on the history of atheism, he interviewed Richard Dawkins and the two discussed the relationship between spirituality and religion. As Dawkins put it: 'I probably do have feelings which may very well be akin to a mystical wonder – when we contemplate the stars, when we contemplate the galaxies, when we contemplate life, the sheer expanse of geological time, I experience … internal feelings which sound pretty much like what mystics feel, and they call it God. And I've been called a religious person for that reason. If I *am* called a religious person, then my retort is you're playing with words, because what the vast majority of people mean by religious is something utterly different from this sort of mystical, transcendent experience. What *they* mean is an entity which interferes in the world, which actually has some kind of impact upon the world, and therefore is a scientific hypothesis. The transcendent, *mystic* sense – that people who are both religious and non-religious, in my usage of the term – is something very, very different.'

Many, perhaps most people experience times when it seems as if the sense of self they normally experience is somehow extended. Listening to music or contemplating the wonders of nature, for example, gives them a sensation of being in touch with another world, a spiritual realm. For people with religious faith, these experiences confirm their belief in the supernatural. Some cannot understand how atheists can have a spiritual life. But many people without religious beliefs describe rich and varied spiritual lives in no way different from those of religious people. They are not denied such experiences. Even church architecture and sacred music may be a source of great pleasure as well as spiritual solace to atheists, as they clearly were to my friend Mary Warnock.

For religious people, these spiritual experiences play an important part in validating their faith. They are confirmed in their beliefs that there is another realm of reality which provides meaning to their lives. Such meaning provides what might be termed universal significance to their existence. They feel part of some larger, though perhaps unknowable purpose. My friends without religious beliefs did not see spiritual experience in this way. They were persuaded by the arguments of neuroscientists such as Sam Harris that spiritual experiences can be explained using naturalistic explanations. Much neuroscience linking brain processes to spirituality has focused on the practice of meditation, with its emphasis on awareness of the present moment and the subduing of the negative mind. Spiritual meditation is sometimes thought of as a means of connecting with a higher power, with God, but it is also widely practiced to gain access to the sort of transcendent experiences described by Richard Dawkins. Such meditation has been found to be linked to the brain's midline regions, especially the medial prefrontal cortex and the medial parietal cortex. Naturalistic explanations such as this do not rule out the possibility of a divine being but make the existence of such a being unnecessary to understanding spirituality and spiritual experience.

Question 8. How can people without religious belief find meaning in their lives?

For people with fundamentalist religious beliefs, the meaning of life lies in the need to fulfil a higher purpose, to act according to God's will. This is achieved by leading a life that conforms to the requirements laid down by religious teaching. Admittedly, many people who belong to one of the organised religions struggle to find a meaning in life despite their beliefs, but they can always and often do fall back on the teaching of their religion as a guide. The fact that most of my friends lacked religious beliefs did not stop them asking themselves fundamental questions about the point of existence. If we are not here to serve the purpose of some supernatural power, they asked themselves, why *are* we here? Necessarily, just as religious teaching begins with a story, their non-religious beliefs also began with a story. What follows is such a story and represents my own attempt to make sense of the discussions I had with some of them while they were alive.

This story begins with the idea that the only meanings we have are those we create for ourselves. These meanings do not, like religious stories, have universal significance but this does not indicate a lack of importance to those who think them. None of my now dead friends behaved as if their lives were meaningless. They thought of their families and friends, their work, their interests and their memories as giving meaning to their lives. That is how they thought and that is the way they behaved. Those who were conscious in their last few weeks and in possession of their faculties, talked to those closest to them not only about the past but about the future and what it held for those who would survive them. The fact that, for them, because of their lack of religious faith, they did not accept a meaning for the universe, was not a matter for regret or disappointment.

Question 9. What difference does belief/non-belief make to the end of life?

There is one significant difference in the last weeks and days of life between religious and non-religious people at least as far as the Abrahamic religions are concerned. The religious beliefs of fundamentalist (but only fundamentalist) Jews, Christians and Muslims all include an afterlife the nature of which depends on how good or badly behaved the person was during their lifetime. Christians, especially those who belong to one or other of the Catholic churches, have the most specific beliefs in this respect. Those who have led a good life will go to Heaven to enjoy the delights of paradise; those who have seriously sinned unless they have shown penance and been absolved for their sins shortly before death by a Christian minister will suffer the torments of Hell in perpetuity while those for whom there is doubt will go to Purgatory until their final fate is decided. Christians further believe that a heartfelt confession before death of all one's sins to an ordained minister combined with a plea for absolution will result in avoidance of the torments of Hell, even for the serious sinner.

Muslims put less emphasis on the possibility of active punishment in an afterlife and instead threaten exclusion from the delights of paradise for those who have sinned, especially those who have committed one of the three most serious sins – murder; idolatry or apostasy; and pre-marital or extra-marital sexual relationships. The afterlife is less clearly laid out for Jews, but the prayers said on The Day of Atonement leave little room for doubt that it is of great importance for their afterlife that Jews pray for forgiveness for the sins they have committed. I learned during my childhood that the fathers of Jewish boys take responsibility for the sins of their sons until they have been barmitzvah after which boys are responsible for themselves. I still have vague memories of the Day of Atonement that occurred a few days after my own barmitzvah during which I confessed to large numbers of sins including those 'for which we incur the penalty of the four forms of capital punishment executed by the Court: stoning, burning, decapitation and strangulation'. Today, many adherents to one or other of the Abrahamic religions in the western world do not take literally these beliefs about the afterlife and the degree to which behaviour in this world affects our chances in the next. But, particularly among those who hold fundamentalist beliefs, they are taken very seriously indeed.

A lack of religious belief does not discourage terminally ill people from looking back over their own lives and finding much to regret, much about which to feel guilty or ashamed. All the same, the institutional insistence on concentrating the mind on matters for regret, shame and guilt and the need for penance among believers in one of the Abrahamic religions makes me grateful my last days will not be burdened in this way. I suspect other non-believers will feel the same.

Whatever our religious beliefs, during our terminal illnesses we are likely to want to be close to our family members, especially our husbands, wives, partners if we have one and, beyond our partners, to our children and grandchildren if we have them, and our friends. Similarly, they are likely to want to be close to us. For those without religious belief, whose commitment is given entirely to those with whom they have formed relationships on this earth, this is clearly more the case than it is for religious people for whom dying is the point at which their relationship with God takes on its most significant importance. This is not to suggest that religious people are less connected to their family members and friends. Far from it! Among my late friends, the small number who were religious were very strongly attached to their children who stayed with them and provided emotional support until the very end. But, inevitably, the paramount need of terminally ill Christian believers to make peace before death with their Creator turns the mind towards the self that seeks salvation and so, at least to some degree, away from others.

Whether believers or not, the pain of permanent separation from loved ones, is likely to be the most emotionally distressing experience for both dying people and their families. Because death so often involves release from physical discomfort, sometimes very severe discomfort, dying may be a more emotionally distressing event for a partner or friend than it is for the person who is dying for whom the prospect of an end to suffering may be most welcome. Not too long after his operation to remove the cancer of his colon, at a time when the rest of his family desperately wanted him to survive, one of my friends declared 'If this is living, then I've had enough of it', and shortly afterwards, he died. This may also be why, when, in places where it is permitted, terminally ill people opt for an assisted death, their relatives often show resistance. They cannot bring themselves to say a final goodbye when the dying person is only too ready to do so.

Both for those who hold religious beliefs and for those who are agnostic or atheist, the last few weeks and days of a terminally ill person are very likely to involve a coming together of close family members and, to a lesser degree, friends. This was true for every single one of my friends who have died over the last decade or so. Children of the terminally ill person visited frequently, often, towards the end, staying the night so that they would not miss the final moments. Some children travelled very long distances from other continents to be with their families at this time. In the final weeks and months, emotional support to the dying person and to their partner or spouse is shown by the presence of loved ones in the home, hospital or hospice, often by the bedside. Precious time may be passed listening to music together, reading favourite passages from novels, books of poetry, recalling good times in the past or musing about the future. When verbal communication is no longer possible, touching, stroking or holding hands are ways of showing emotional support.

It is sometimes thought that the existence of rituals which mark the end of the life of a religious believer, the visit of a Christian minister to hear a confession, the utterance of a final Hebrew prayer, the expression by a devout Muslim that Allah is the only God, - all these are comforting and denied the atheist or non-believer. None of my late friends complained of the absence of a final ritual before their deaths. Most were 'going gentle', asleep or in a coma for at least some time before they died. Some of those left behind after a death, did indeed regret the absence of some form of ritual to mark the passing of a loved one. But the great majority found comfort in talking to each other about the death as a release from suffering, about their feelings of love for the person who had died and about the different ways the dead person would be remembered and thus live on until those who had known him or her had, in their turn, met the ultimate fate of all of us. These are good ways to die and good ways to be remembered.

Question 10. Is it normal to feel anxious about dying/death?

My recollection is that, while not exactly afraid of death, while lying in my Swiss hospital bed, I was indeed alarmed at the thought that I might die. I was, after all, not yet sixty. I was facing the loss of the rest of my life which I might reasonably have expected to last another twenty or so years. This made me feel disappointed rather than anxious or fearful. My late friends, when terminally ill, were in a different situation. They were all in their late seventies or, much more commonly, in their eighties. Although a small number of them did have a little hope of some sort of existence after death, the great majority thought that, after death, they would live on only in the memories of those they had known in life.

The probability or, in most cases, the certainty of total oblivion after death that most of my friends anticipated might, in contrast, seem an appalling prospect. Certainly, the poet, Philip Larkin, thought so. He wrote in his often-quoted poem *Aubade*:

' ... the total emptiness for ever,
The sure extinction that we travel to
And shall be lost in always. Not to be here,
Not to be anywhere,
And soon; nothing more terrible, nothing more true.
... – no sight, no sound,
No touch or taste or smell, nothing to think with,
Nothing to love or link with,
The anaesthetic from which none come round.
And so it stays just on the edge of vision,
A small unfocused blur, a standing chill
That slows each impulse down to indecision.
Most things may never happen: this one will.'

Aubade was first published in the 1977 Christmas edition of the Times Literary Supplement. It has retained its grip on the imagination to this day. The playwright, Harold Pinter, used to recite it regularly at Christmas family gatherings. As revealed in Andrew Motion's biography, Larkin retained a crippling fear of death until his own dying day and other writers have echoed his sentiment. Julian Barnes, the novelist, declares 'For me, death is the one appalling fact which defines life; unless you are constantly aware of it, you cannot begin to understand what life is about …' (p.126). But many, perhaps most people who lack belief in an afterlife do not take such a bleak view of their own extinction. At the other extreme from Larkin and Barnes, Rabindranath Tagore, the Nobel Prize winning poet from a Hindu background, wrote how he welcomed death.

'Death, thy servant, is at my door … The night is dark and my heart is fearful –yet I will take up the lamp, open my gates and bow to him my welcome … I will worship him with folded hands, and with tears. I will worship him placing at his feet the treasure of my heart'.

Similar thoughts were expressed by Karen Lewis in response to a request by Humanists UK to members to describe how they felt about death.

'I wouldn't want to live forever. The certainty of death is my friend. A friend who helps me lead a good life, helps me to laugh and cry, to love, to take a risk, motivates me to be brave and say yes to experiences whilst I can… It is painful to think of my loved ones in grief and I worry about the challenges they will face as they inherit this messy planet. I hope I will live through them as they inherit my behaviours and traits – hopefully the good ones! I am certain my legacy will be remembered through them, so I'm trying to make good memories and to tread lightly on this earth for the fleeting time I am lucky enough to be here.'

Perhaps surprisingly, none of my interviewees, reported that the family member who had died had been seriously anxious about dying in the weeks or months before the event. A few days before he died, one was reported to be 'a little scared' but mainly relieved, because, as a result of his physical symptoms, he so wanted to die. None of my other friends were reported to show signs of anxiety about death, though many were distressed or agitated as a result of their physical symptomatology. As I have indicated, one of the main reasons, (perhaps the most important reason) why my friends showed so little anxiety about death was their age. It is noteworthy that even in the knowledge of their impending deaths, they largely remained free from death anxiety.

Ernest Becker, an American cultural anthropologist, has been perhaps the most influential voice writing about death anxiety. In *The Denial of Death,* he contrasted two views about fear of death: His preferred view was that the fear of death is natural and affects everyone; it is the basic fear that influences all others. Fear of death rarely shows its face but underneath all appearances, it is universally present. Evolutionary theory, as I have already described, sees death as a biological and evolutionary necessity. In general, the experiences of my friends supports Becker's view that fear of death is uncommon among people who have had a loving, affectionate upbringing. There was very little evidence of any repression of death anxiety among my friends. None had suffered severe mental illness. (A number had dementia, but this is a disorder of the brain not thought to arise from repressed emotion). A small number had received courses of psychotherapy, either as part of their professional training or for mild episodes of depression brought on by stress. It is not that they were in any way indifferent to death, either in themselves or in others. Until death became inevitable, they submitted themselves to medical or surgical treatment, even when this had most unpleasant side-effects. A number continued to agree to such treatment even when the chances of cure or even a significant period of remission, were slim.

A small number of family members told me of the belief among orthodox Jews that life and death are in the hands of God, and that it was wrong to attempt to interfere with divine will in this respect. This was given as the reason why there are no Jewish hospices in the UK, these being places where health professionals interfere with the divine will. However, there are Jewish hospices in New York, Amsterdam and Israel, so clearly this is not a universal belief among Jewish people. Further, such a belief seemed to play no part in the decisions about treatment taken by my friends who were of Jewish origin, though a small number were aware of it. Indeed, a number of my Jewish friends spent their last weeks and days in hospices run by professionals with a strong Christian ethos.

Question 11. What are we anxious about losing when we die?

Fear is mainly about loss. We fear we will lose what we have or what we might have in the future. And death, for most of us, involves the loss of pretty well everything. This sense of loss in terminal illness includes a sense of what others will lose by one's demise. A long-standing partner will lose a life companion and all the pleasure that goes with shared experiences. Empathy with this sense of loss that others will experience on one's death may be a cardinal feature of feelings that come with dying. In contrast, for those with certain religious beliefs the loss that comes with death will be amply compensated by knowledge that one is about to enter the Kingdom of Heaven. But, as we shall see later, even among those with religious beliefs, certainty that there is an afterlife is now only experienced by a minority of those living in western societies.

Question 12. Why have I lived?

As I lay in my hospital bed, other questions came to mind. In particular, I asked myself the question 'Why have I lived?' or what had been the meaning of my life. While asking for the meaning of life in a general sense has often been regarded by philosophers as a meaningless question or one to which there is no meaningful answer, asking oneself what has been the point of one's own life seems a perfectly reasonable, if perhaps a rather brave thing to do. I thought in Switzerland, as I do now, that the meaning or purpose of my life is best understood by reflecting on each of my many role identities. This notion of role identity provides one answer and, for me, the least unsatisfactory answer to the question why we exist if it is not, as religious people believe, for some higher purpose. Others might find a consideration of the way one has achieved fulfilment through the various roles one has performed as a helpful way of reviewing one's past life.

An identity is a sense of who one is as an individual as well as a sense of how others see us. A sense of who one is comes with an experience of being in a role in which one is expected to behave in particular ways. So role identities are both personally and socially defined. Reviewing the number of identities I have experienced during my life, I am astonished at the number there are or have been. Over the years, I have been a son, grandson, nephew, brother, husband, lover, friend, neighbour, schoolboy, fighter controller (during my National Service), medical student, doctor, child psychiatrist, medical academic, teacher, researcher, writer, biographer, tourist, member of the Labour Party, secular Jew, atheist, north Londoner, middle class, British, English, European, old man, supporter of Arsenal Football Club, supporter of Luton Town Football Club. It is through my role identities that I have experienced fulfilment as a person.

Some of these thirty role identities (and there could be others I have forgotten) are, for me, only historical. At the age of ninety, it is naturally many, many years since I had an identity as a grandson though I still have a recollection of what it felt like to be a grandson. Some identities are much weaker in their influence than others. The football teams I support generally only have my weak allegiance but, at the time of writing, Luton Town has just been promoted to the Premier League for the first time in their history, so my identity with this club has suddenly increased. Without doubt, my strongest current role identities are those that arise from my family but if one measures the importance of an identity by the amount of time spent in activity related to it, then, at the moment, being a writer is a very strong part of my self. This book would never get written if this were not the case.

For much of my life, my work or occupational identity has rivalled in strength my various family identities. This is the case for perhaps the majority of men of my generation. For women of my generation and certainly for the generation that preceded it, their family identities as wives, mothers and daughters will usually have given them their strongest sense of who they are or have been - their identities. There is sometimes a marked difference between one's personal and one's social identity. For example, I do not feel myself intellectually or emotionally to be an old man. But when I walk in the nearby park, I know that when those who pass by take one look at me walking rather unsteadily, using a stick or Nordic poles, they perceive me to be an old, indeed a very old man.

The meaning of our own lives, especially as we get older, derives at least partly, from the recall of identities we have had in the past. These memories of past identities and of how we performed them help to give our current existence meaning. That is why dementia is so tragic, as memory loss removes our capacity to find meanings derived from our past lives (see Chapter 7).

The development of identities

As someone whose professional work as a child psychiatrist has involved constant observation of the way infants develop into children and children into adolescents and then adults, I have naturally thought of the way our identities develop, evolve and continue to provide us with a sense of meaning. Our first identities are chosen for us. As new-born babies, our first overriding motivation, the point of life, is to survive. That is why babies are programmed to search for and suck at the breast or bottle, and their mothers are programmed to ensure a ready supply of milk. Babies rapidly learn that their survival depends on the continued existence of their mothers. For babies, the possibility that their mother will not survive is their first intimation of mortality. For a baby, when a mother has left the room, as far as it knows, she has gone forever. This means that, from the start, mortality is inextricably linked to the existence of the 'other'.

Thus, the point of living becomes, in one's infancy and afterwards, the ensuring that the 'other', on whom one depends, continues to exist. The identity of this important 'other' changes from being exclusively the mother, to include a number of 'others', including father, siblings and friends. It is for these people that we first experience not just affection, longing and soon love, but also the desire, in return, to be longed for and loved. For many people, on falling in love or making a deep attachment, these 'others' crystallise into one person. This important 'other' is likely to be a partner or spouse. The purpose or meaning of living then becomes bound up with the existence of the one 'other', who may well not be unequivocally loved, indeed about whom one's feelings may be ambivalent or even hostile. Nevertheless, it is this 'other' who gives meaning to life. The terminal illness of the 'other' threatens to remove the meaning life has for a partner. This is surely what grief is about. Thus death, although it marks the end of an individual life, is also an event of massive social significance. Consequently, terminal illness is a social as well as an individual threat. Doctors, nurses and others are trained to see dying and death as purely individual events, though some broaden their vision so that they see death as involving, in addition, the demise of one or more social relationships.

Of course, this does not mean that people who do not have a significant 'other' are unable to find meaning in their lives. Meaning derives from many identities other than being a partner. But it happens that nearly all my close friends who recently died did indeed have one relationship that was especially important in giving their lives meaning. This was the case for all but two, - one woman who never married and one who was a widow for the last thirty years of her life. Both these women regarded themselves as having led full lives, as full and meaningful as any of the others.

Now to return to the development of role identities. After a few months of life, babies become conscious of themselves as individuals, separate from others. It is at this point that they develop identities which, for the first time, give their lives meaning. The blind drive to survive is replaced by a sense of meaning for existence which is found in behaving in ways that emerge from our identities, the ideas of who we are. Such identities are at the core of our being. They are our essence. Our first identities are those that emerge because of our role in our family of origin. We are the child of our parents. Very soon afterwards, this role is merged with that of our gender so that we are more than a child – we are a daughter or a son, Gender identity is the first identity we have that is separate from our family position and it is of major importance. Perhaps this is why feelings about transgender are so intense. To these first identities of family position and gender are rapidly added others, some again emerging from our place in our families. So, we become sisters or brothers, grandchildren, nephews, nieces, cousins. Then, outside the family, we become a friend of one or more other children. As with the identities we assume later on, some of these family and friendship identities are highly salient to the way we think of ourselves, others only faintly so. The level of salience depends on the strength of the attachment to the people or ideas that form part of the particular identity. As we move through primary and secondary education into occupations, our identities multiply. We may become affiliated to our local football team, to our city, country, religion or ethnic group. By the time we are in our twenties, we are likely to have at least twenty identities each of which requires us to behave in a particular way. Instead of 'I think therefore I am' most of us tell ourselves 'I am a daughter/son/student. I am a friend, I am white British or whatever: therefore I am.' It is not thinking that gives us a sense of existence; it is who we think we are.

Further, our role identities do not just give us a sense of self, they provide us with 'scripts' that guide us to behave in particular ways. My late friend, John Gagnon, an American sociologist, in conjunction with a colleague, William Simon, developed a highly influential theory in the 1970s to explain sexual behaviour. But sexual script theory is applicable to all types of behaviour, not just sexual behaviour. It takes account of the way cultural beliefs interact with the previous personal experience of an individual and the way those with whom the individual themselves behave to explain why people behave in one way rather than another. The theory provides a bridge between awareness of a particular identity and the behaviour of an individual, between, for example, a person's identity as a daughter and the sort of filial behaviour a daughter shows, influenced by societal expectations of how daughters should behave, her previous experience with her parent, and the way the parent reacts to her behaviour.

The point of this long digression into our multiple role identities is to suggest that when each of us reflects, as life comes to a close, on the meaning of our existence, one helpful way of organising our thoughts may be to consider our roles in each of the many identities we have or have had in the past. In our families, we have all at least been sons or daughter, but then, later in our lives, we have taken on many more family identities. Our working lives have, in all probability, given us more identities. What has been the purpose of these? Outside family and work, we may well have performed other roles, which have fulfilled other purposes. I would suggest an uncritical self-appraisal may provide some meaning, coherence and, in the end, comfort and understanding to those who are terminally ill.

Question 13. How did my friends find meaning in their lives?

Most of my late friends, as I knew them, had two main sets of identities. The first set related to their different roles in their families. Initially as sons or daughters, then (in all but one case), as wives or husbands and then (again in all but one case), as parents. (One never married or had children but nevertheless had a major family role identity as an aunt to her niece). The second set of identities related to their work or occupation. For most, this occupational identity remained stable throughout their working lives, but for others, there was a change (sometimes a marked change) in work identity. Thus, one retired as soon as she could from her work as a university academic child psychiatrist, to take up voluntary work advocating for children whose lives had been destroyed in war zones. Two of my friends, who had been solicitors, gave up rewarding private practice to enter the public sector. One became a taxing master, adjudicating on the appropriateness of legal fees. Another solicitor also gave up private practice to become an ombudsman. A friend who had been a journalist and then a producer of high-quality BBC radio programmes analysing current politics, went into BBC administration. Another friend moved from being a financial journalist on *The Financial Times*, to running small and sometimes not so small businesses. Mary Warnock gave up her job as a moral philosopher in an Oxford college to become the headmistress of an independent girls' school, finishing up as Mistress of a Cambridge college. Jonathan Miller who started his working life as an NHS doctor, became an actor and then a director of operas, plays, films and BBC documentaries. Nearly all my friends found great satisfaction in their identities, both their family identities and their occupational identities which gave meaning to their lives. An exception was Jonathan Miller who frequently went on record as regretting his departure from medicine and neuroscience.

Other thoughts

There were other questions I asked myself in my Swiss hospital bed, but these shall remain private. I hope however that the expression I have given to the questions that I asked myself in my hospital bed may stimulate others to ask themselves questions, doubtless mainly different ones, about matters on which they would like to reflect in their final weeks and months.

CHAPTER 3

The nature of terminal illnesses

Readers with a health background will probably wish to skip all or most of this and the following chapter as they are unlikely to contain information which they do not already know.

Introduction

Thou know'st, t'is common, all that lives must die, Passing through nature to eternity. (Hamlet, Act 1, Scene 2)

People without religion will all agree with the first line of Hamlet's reflection on death while rejecting the second line as a fantasy. They would also surely agree with Hamlet's later meditation on the wonderful nature of the human body: 'What a piece of work is man!' (Act 2, Scene 2). Indeed, the extraordinarily complex nature of the human mind and body has been used as an argument for the existence of God. Now termed 'intelligent design', this asserts that the biological features of the human body are too complex to have arisen as a result of natural selection and must have come about through the work of a divine intelligence.

Other religious explanations of death are well-known and in sharp contrast to the views of evolutionary biologists discussed in Chapter 2. Christianity explains that humans forfeited immortality in the Garden of Eden as a result of Eve's sin and that the punishment for this sin has been transmitted down the generations. The death of Jesus Christ, however, made possible the salvation of the souls of repentant Christians. According to Islamic belief, death is a beautiful gift, making possible a transition to a far better world. While Jews do not appear to have an explanation for death, they do believe in a life after death - the immortality of the soul and the physical resurrection of the body at a time in the future. Hindus believe that the body is a temporary vessel for an immortal soul in the mortal realm. When we die, our physical body perishes but our soul lives on. They believe that death simply leads to rebirth. Buddhists have a belief in reincarnation – that, after death, a person's spirit remains close by and seeks out a new body and new life.

Since the publication in 1859 of Charles Darwin's *Theory of Evolution*, which dealt, for many, a death blow to all these religious explanations of mortality, there have been further advances in scientific understanding of the adaptive significance of a limited span of life. In his two books, *The Selfish Gene* and *The Blind Watchmaker*, Richard Dawkins, the evolutionary biologist, in particular, using recent developments in genetic science, has pointed to the way random mutations bringing improvements in survival are passed on to future generations in preference to genes that do not contain such mutations.

While it may be an exaggeration to assert, as some have, that death is the primary tool of evolution, it is true that evolutionary change could not occur without it. Human immortality would mean the species was stuck with the genes it has now, embedded in an increasingly aged population. The fact that, like artefacts such as electric light bulbs and motor cars, we have built-in obsolescence, permits changes in human development that would not otherwise be possible. There are, of course, evolutionary disadvantages to death. The wise elderly cannot directly pass on their wisdom. but books can immortalise such wisdom, even if their originators pass on. At least, unlike most artefacts, our bodies are made up of biodegradable waste and do not pollute the planet when we die.

Ways of slowing the ageing process

You can't stop ageing. How rapidly you age is largely down to luck, - especially how lucky you have been in the genes you have inherited. But the life you lead, your lifestyle, will have some influence on the speed with which you age and your likelihood of getting seriously ill. In this chapter, I shall first describe what we can do to slow, though not stop the ageing processes. I shall then go on to consider the functions of the different organs of our bodies and how these can go wrong in ways that threaten our lives. Finally, I shall describe the medical and surgical interventions that can reduce our likelihood of dying but that will, in the end, not be able to prevent death in any of us.

Smoking

Don't smoke anything. They are your lungs but that's my advice. If you've smoked cigarettes in the past, you are at higher risk of various chronic health problems and of premature death. If you are smoking now, these risks are higher. Stopping smoking is difficult but very much worth it if you value your health and want to live longer. The health risks of smoking nicotine are higher than the risks of vaping or smoking cannabis which are less well established but probably present.

Diet

After not smoking, not putting on weight is the best thing you can do for your health. Learn how to calculate your Body Mass Index (BMI). If at all possible, keep your BMI below 25. If your BMI is above 25, then adjust your diet to bring it below that figure. In the end, it's the amount you eat that determines your weight. You should certainly take exercise (see below) but you won't lose weight just exercising. Losing weight is difficult but a few tips may be helpful.

- Experts don't tell you this. Of course, it is how much you eat that matters but there is *great variation* between us in how actively we burn up calories. Some people can eat a vast amount without putting on weight; for others even a relatively low-calorie intake can result in obesity. If you are in the latter category, you just have to accept your fate; food intake has to be very limited.

- Salt, sugar and alcohol are the main drivers making us put on weight.

- Don't go on a rapid weight reduction course. You will put back on the weight you have lost much more rapidly than if you've lost weight slowly.

- Don't snack. Keep your fridge and cupboards empty of foods that are bad for you. You are less likely to snack if you have to go out to buy something.

- Weigh yourself only once a week. Daily weighing is likely to be misleading.

Exercise

Taking regular, or almost daily exercise is the key. The main benefits of taking regular exercise are that it keeps your muscles from wasting and your joints from seizing up. If you take your heart for a walk, it is much less likely to lose its capacity to pump blood efficiently round your body. Exercise also makes you feel better and prevents depression It won't lose you much, if any weight. This means the exercise you do should be exercise you really enjoy. This might be going for a walk or jogging (not good for your joints) or Pilates or Yoga or using an exercise bike to the sound of music. Swimming is good too, but involves a whole paraphernalia of going somewhere, getting undressed, putting on a costume or trunks and showering and getting dressed again afterwards. Enough to put me off, but maybe not you. It is particularly important that you resume exercise as soon as possible if you are off your feet for more than a few days. As you age, your muscles waste away remarkably rapidly if you do not use them.

Maintaining a healthy blood pressure

Keeping your blood pressure within normal limits reduces your likelihood of having a stroke or heart attack. There are two measurements that are relevant – a higher one called the systolic and a lower one called the diastolic. The difference between them is your 'pulse pressure'. If you are less than 75 a blood pressure around 140 (systolic) and 80 (diastolic) or lower is about right. Over 80 years, then 150 over 90 or lower is probably better. If your blood pressure is consistently over these numbers, you probably need to be taking antihypertensive medication, like just under half the elderly population, so consult your doctor. If it is consistently over 20 points above the recommended numbers, then go to see a doctor about it straightaway. You can buy a machine for measuring blood pressure relatively cheaply. To begin with, take your blood pressure two or three times a day for four or five days and note the numbers. If the average readings are within normal limits, then only take it once a month after that. If you are over the recommended numbers, then work out with your doctor the doses of medication you need. Once you've established satisfactory levels, then again, taking your blood pressure once a month is quite sufficient. If your blood pressure is too low, you might have fainting attacks in which you feel you have to sit or lie down. If this happens, consult your doctor who may think you need to be reducing your anti-hypertensive medication.

Hearing

Some loss of hearing is almost universal as we get older. It is likely to show itself first in not being able to hear in crowded places like restaurants in which there is a lot of background noise. Get your hearing checked once every two years. Poor hearing is a risk factor for dementia, so make sure you do this. If hearing aids are recommended, then do get them and wear them regularly. They take some getting used to but it's worth it.

Vision

Get your eyes checked once every two years or every year if you notice some deterioration in your vision. The optometrist will tell you not only if you need to wear or change spectacles but whether you need an operation for cataract. About half the population over 75 have cataract but its presence does not mean you need an operation. Your optometrist will tell you when this looks necessary.

Teeth

About a quarter of the population over the age of 75 wear complete or partial sets of dentures. If you get your teeth checked regularly at six monthly or yearly intervals you are less likely to need dentures.

Feet

Cut your toenails or, if you can't reach them, get someone else to cut them regularly. Keep the skin of your feet and ankles moist by using moisturisers daily. If you have a fungus infection between your toes spray on surgical spirit regularly. A regular appointment with an NHS chiropodist/podiatrist to check on your feet and remove corns etc is a good idea, but if you can't find one and can afford it, do go privately.

The expense of keeping your body in as good order as possible

Some of this costs money which you may or may not have. But some can come free. A healthy diet need not cost more than an unhealthy one, though it may be more difficult to buy. Regular walking does not cost. How much it costs to look after your hearing, vision, teeth and feet will depend on how comprehensive the NHS provision is for your area. If you can possibly afford it however, you should not hesitate to spend money on keeping your body in good shape.

Our bodies

For some readers the summary of human anatomy and physiology which follows will seem superfluous or even felt to be insulting, but I'm pretty sure for others it will contain useful, even new information. I write this because when I was eighteen, I decided to give up my university place to read law and to study medicine instead. Up to that time, I had had no science education at all. Consequently, I had no idea how my body worked. I clearly remember that I thought, for example, that after food entered my mouth it descended into a sort of churn which rolled it around for a while before the bits it didn't need came out at the other end. It was news to me that there was a very long tube from my mouth to my anus and that there was a rather complicated process of extraction of nutrients until my faeces were expelled. If I had pursued a legal career, though apparently highly educated, I would probably have retained this false belief about my insides throughout my life.

The brain is the central, organising part of our body. It is responsible for our speech and language, our ability to control our movements, our capacity to make judgements and decisions, our perception of the visual world, of sounds, tastes, smells and touch. Part of the brain controls our balance. At the base of the brain before it tapers down into the spinal cord are the lower brain centres responsible for control of the vital functions of respiration and blood circulation.

Above all, the brain is the seat of consciousness, that part of us that allows us to be aware not only of our existence but of our numerous identities. Despite major advances in recent years in the neurosciences, we still have very little idea how mind or mental activity arises from the physical activity of the brain. Maybe our brains are not up to this task and we never will. We have much better understanding of the way some of the nerves that emerge from the spinal cord control our movements and how other nerves are responsible for sending messages about our sensations from our fingers, hands, arms, feet and legs back to the brain.

Although the brain functions as a whole, different parts of the brain do have special functions.

a) Frontal lobes. These are responsible for organisation, planning, problem-solving and decision-making. If you are right-handed, the expression of speech and language centres are in the left frontal (dominant) lobe, as well as in the left temporal lobe, vice versa if you are left-handed.

b) Parietal lobes. These integrate the information provided by the five senses (taste, touch, smell, hearing and vision). The dominant parietal lobe processes the comprehension of language while the non-dominant lobe (the right in right-handed people) deals with orientation in space.

c) Occipital lobes. Situated at the back of the brain, these receive messages from the eyes and are responsible for our capacity to distinguish shapes and visual patterns.

d)   Temporal lobes. These deal with messages from the ears and, together with the dominant parietal lobe, enable us to comprehend language. It is also the seat of most short-term memory.

e)   Cerebellum. This is the organ of balance.

f)   Brain stem. Situated at the base of the brain, this is where the central control of our so-called vital functions, breathing, blood pressure and heart rate takes place.

g)   Thalamus and hypothalamus. This central part of the brain controls temperature as well as the secretion of our hormones.

h)   Ventricles. These are spaces in the interior of the brain that contain cerebro-spinal fluid.

i)   Lining of the brain. Surrounding the brain are the meninges, a membrane which lines the inside of the skull in which the brain is situated.

The intestinal tract is the tube that runs from your mouth to your anus via the pharynx (throat), oesophagus (gullet), stomach, small intestine, large intestine and rectum. Each part of the intestinal tract may be the site of a cancer or a blockage or a bleed or an infection or a mixture of these. The commonest symptoms are vomiting, abdominal pain, diarrhoea, constipation and bleeding from the mouth or anus.

The heart is best viewed as a collapsible bag of muscle which pumps blood around the body - a vital function because the blood contains oxygen, a chemical element without which none of the other organs would function.

The blood leaves the heart in gradually narrowing tubes called arteries. These continue as narrower tubes called arterioles which then narrow further to become really tiny capillary vessels. When the oxygen has been extracted from the capillaries by the various organs to which it is distributed, the deoxygenated blood is returned to the heart in tubes called veins. The blood is then pumped by the heart into the lungs where it meets the air we breathe and is reoxygenated. This oxygen-rich blood is then pumped back to the heart for circulation round the rest of the body. The heart is divided into four chambers which inter-connect by holes through which the blood passes from one chamber to another. Each hole is guarded by a valve which regulates the blood flow. Valves may be malformed from birth (congenital valve disease) or become damaged with time as you age.

The kidneys share with our bowels the task of ridding the body of waste materials. The arteries bring waste material to the two kidneys where it is filtered and sent down tubes called ureters to the bladder. When we urinate, the urine passes from the bladder down another tube called the urethra through, in men, the penis, into the toilet. Surrounding the urethra in men is a rather useless organ called the prostate, notable only because it is the site of a high proportion of male cancers. In women, the urethra passes in front of the womb and ovaries, again both common sites for cancers, though with distinctly more important functions than the prostate gland. You have two kidneys, one on either side in your lower back region. This is lucky as if one kidney goes out of action, the other one is usually sufficient to clear the body of the waste products that are expelled in the urine. The most common diseases affecting the kidneys are infections and cancers. The ureters, the tubes running from the kidneys to the bladder may become blocked by infection or cancers which are also the types of disease affecting the bladder itself. The prostate is an organ men have that surrounds the urethra, a tube running from the bladder through the penis to the outside world which may also be affected by infection or cancer.

Though women are not at risk from cancer of the prostate, they do have *breasts*. Developing in size at puberty, with the production of milk their only function, they account for over half the cancers in women.

The liver is a large organ situated in the upper right of the abdomen under the ribs. Its main function is to filter the blood and process carbohydrates, proteins and fats so that they are more readily available to serve the body's needs. It removes toxic substances like alcohol that might be harmful to the body. It also produces bile that passes to the gall bladder and then into the intestinal tract. Finally, it produces proteins important in blood clotting.

The lungs are large organs in the chest which expand when you breathe in and contract when you breathe out. This is where the transfer of oxygen from the outside air to the blood in the arteries takes place as well as the reverse – the removal of carbon dioxide from the veins. Any failure of these transfers because, for example, of infection or heart failure or cancer, results in lack of availability of oxygen to the body. This causes struggling for breath and, if severe, will inevitably prove fatal. The body cannot function without oxygen. Some potentially fatal lung conditions are caused by smoking. These include some forms of lung cancer and chronic obstructive pulmonary disease (COPD).

The endocrine glands secrete hormones into your blood system that are essential for a variety of functions. Hormones are chemicals that coordinate different functions of your body by sending messages via your blood to different organs. Of your endocrine glands, the most likely to cause trouble are the pancreas and the thyroid. The pancreas is tucked into the liver, next to the gall bladder. It secretes insulin which controls your blood sugar level (see below). The thyroid is located in front of your larynx (voice box), in your throat. It controls your metabolic rate, the speed at which food is transformed into energy.

Other organs not covered above include the tonsils, spleen, appendix, skin, lymph glands, muscles, tendons and joints. All of these may give rise to illnesses that may prove terminal.

Terminal Illnesses

Whilst most people, like many of our friends, can expect the very last days of their lives to be relatively free of pain and suffering as they slip into coma before they die, the same cannot be said of our terminal illnesses. Except for the minority of sudden deaths, these will characteristically last several months or years. As the stories of the last illnesses of my friends reveal, serious physical discomfort and uncertainty over the outcome are the rule rather than the exception.

So, what are the causes of our deaths? We die because one or more of our bodily organs stops working. Usually, more than one organ fails at the end, so doctors talk about multi-organ failure. When my elderly friends, (most of whom are not doctors), and I meet, our conversation usually begins with what we call an 'organ recital'. This involves an account of the most recent symptoms we've had and how they've been dealt with. We try to keep this organ recital as short as possible and sometimes we try to ban it altogether.

The conditions from which we die

The friends we have lost over recent years were mainly in their eighties or early nineties. Nine of them died of cancer and six of heart disease. In six, dementia was the main cause of death. Two died of disorders of the blood and two of progressive neurological disorders. These causes of death are fairly typical of those in this age group in the general population. The fact that our friends mostly lived into their eighties is a little unusual and is probably accounted for by the fact that they were all reasonably affluent, were able to afford healthy diets, took at least moderate exercise and, except for two of them, did not smoke.

In the general population as among our friends, the most common causes of terminal illnesses are the cancers. These are diseases in which the body's cells grow uncontrollably, to begin with affecting the organ in which they first appear and then spreading to other parts of the body. Cancer cells destroy normal tissue causing organ failure. Tumours or cancerous swellings also damage the body by creating blockages or obstructions. All types of cancer may spread to other parts of the body forming 'metastases' or secondary tumours, though some are much more likely to do this than others. If you have a cancer, metastases are just as likely to end your life as so-called primary tumours. The most common cancers are those arising in the breast, prostate and bowel, but all organs can be affected by cancer.

The second commonest cause of terminal illness is infection by microscopic bacteria, viruses or, (mainly in hot climates), a variety of other organisms. Again, all organs can be attacked by infections. I am writing in the middle of a pandemic caused by the virus. Covid 19. There has been so much in the news explaining the ways this virus damages human tissues and is spread from person to person that any detailed description would be superfluous. We all now know that people vary in their capacity to resist infections with those who are very old or lacking an effective immune system being the most vulnerable. Before Covid 19, the most common lethal virus was influenza which, before the pandemic, killed tens of thousands of mainly elderly people every winter.

A third important cause of terminal illness are the so-called degenerative diseases. As we age, our blood vessels gradually lose their elasticity and are more likely to get clogged up by deposits of cholesterol. The brain and heart muscle are particularly likely to be affected by a blood supply that is inadequate for this reason. The secretion of insulin, the hormone controlling our blood sugar, becomes less effective with age and many of us develop Type 2 diabetes, the diabetes of older people. This, in itself, is not a common cause of death, but often contributes to other terminal illnesses. Degeneration of the cartilage in our joints means we become stiff and more prone to falls, another important cause of death in the old.

However, by far the most challenging degenerative disease is dementia. Out of the twenty-four friends of mine who have died over the last ten years, six suffered from dementia during their terminal illnesses. It was, without question, the most distressing and problematic feature of their last months or, in one or two cases of their last several years. So, I make no apology for discussing it at greater length later in a separate chapter.

Finally, there is the question whether old age is itself a disease. The issue is controversial. In some parts of the United States, if doctors put 'old age' as a cause of death on a death certificate, it is sent back to them for alteration. There, old age is not allowed to be responsible for death. In Britain, while 'old age' is permissible as a cause of death, most doctors would add another disease as a contributory reason. They should, if they were really accurate, put several. In fact, as we get older, all our organs, without exception, function less well than they did when we were younger.

The Course of Terminal Illness

Stage One. The first symptoms of what turns out to be a terminal illness may straightaway suggest something is seriously wrong. Alternatively, these early symptoms may be rather vague and seem harmless, like tiredness or loss of appetite. In either event, you will want to consult a doctor who will listen to your story and probably order some investigations.

Stage Two. The investigations suggest something serious is going on. Your doctor will discuss what might be the matter and probably refer you to a specialist. The specialist will confirm there is real cause for concern. He or she may be reassuring or warn of a possibly bad outcome or, more likely, indicate there is uncertainty about the future course of the illness. A line of treatment will be proposed usually involving either medical or surgical interventions or both. If the illness is terminal, these interventions may be ineffective or have an uncertain effect.

Stage Three. It becomes clear that the illness has not responded to treatment and is going to shorten life. It is uncertain for just how long life can extend.

Stage Four. The illness has advanced and it is clear that there are only days or weeks to go before the illness proves fatal.

These stages take place at greatly varying speed. An illness may proceed at such a rapid rate that there are only a few weeks or even days between Stage 1 and Stage 4. More commonly there are several months or even years between these two stages.

The strength of the link between the stage the terminally ill person is at from a medical point of view and awareness that the illness is indeed terminal and will end in death varies greatly. An initial symptom that is obviously serious such as bleeding from the bowel or bladder, or a stroke, is likely to be accompanied by an almost immediate awareness that this could be a life-threatening illness. In contrast, a person can go through the first three stages without being aware of a potentially fatal outcome. The symptomatology and information from doctors is only one influence on awareness of the life-threatening nature of an illness. The quality of communication and trust between doctor and patient as well as the personality of the patient are all important influences on such awareness. Of particular importance is the way the individual faces bad news generally, for example with denial or with acceptance or, most probably, with something between the two.

The effects of disease affecting the brain will depend particularly on whether the damage is caused by thrombosis (clotting) or haemorrhage (bleeding) of the arteries supplying the brain or there is disease directly damaging the brain tissue itself. A 'stroke' is an event in which there is a clot in an artery or a bleed that cuts off the blood supply to a part of the brain. The symptoms will depend on which part of the brain is affected. Most commonly there is paralysis down one side of the body and if the dominant side (left for a right-handed person and right for a left-handed person) of the brain is affected then usually there will be loss of speech and understanding of speech. Sometimes the clot will be very small and there will only be temporary loss of function, other parts of the brain taking over. If this happens frequently, the person is said to have suffered a temporary ischaemic attack or a TIA.

Cancers of the brain are relatively common. Sometimes these are primary tumours but more usually they arise from fragments of tumour growing elsewhere in the body being carried by the blood stream up to the brain and taking root there as so-called secondary metastases.

In many ways the most distressing disease of the brain is dementia which is described in Chapter 7.

Investigations

- Blood tests
  Whichever symptoms take you to the doctor, he or she is likely to ask for one or more blood tests. Just very occasionally the result of the blood test will immediately provide a diagnosis. This is the case with the various forms of leukaemia or cancers of the blood cells. More commonly a blood test will only give a general indication of what might be wrong. Often, if the result of the blood test is normal, this is useful as it rules out many lines of further enquiry.

- Imaging

  These investigations may take the form of old-fashioned but sometimes still very informative X-Rays, CT (computerised tomography) or MRI (magnetic resonance imagery) scans. Extra information from an X-Ray can be provided if it is preceded by injection of a dye into the blood stream so that the pictures can reveal more exactly where pathology (disease) lies.

  CT scans produce pictures of cross sections of the organs that are to be visualised. Having a CT scan involves no more discomfort than does an X-Ray. An MRI, on the other hand, requires you to lie in a confined space or tunnel while the images are taken. This can be difficult for people with claustrophobia but usually these can be helped to cooperate sufficiently for images to be obtained.

- Special organ-specific investigations. There is now a wide range of investigations that may be requested depending on the organ that is in question. For example, an echocardiograph will reveal how each chamber of your heart is functioning.

- Investigative surgery

  This can be as simple as having a small sample (a biopsy) of the skin taken to a much more intrusive surgical procedure such as a laparotomy – an operation to open up your abdomen to see what is going on there. Various forms of 'scope' are used to look down your throat into your stomach or up your rectum (back passage) as far as your colon. Bronchoscopes are used to examine the tubes leading to your lungs. Sometimes having a look can be combined with doing a biopsy or a repair as when so-called 'stents' (see below) are inserted into an artery that has been found to be blocked so that the blood can get through more easily.

Medical and surgical interventions

- Treatments for cancer. There are three main lines of treatment for cancer. These can be given alone or in combination:

  a) Chemotherapy. These are drugs that kill cells while they are dividing to form new cells. Because cancer cells divide much more often than normal cells, they are more likely than normal cells to be killed by these drugs. Chemotherapy may be given by an injection into the bloodstream via a vein or by a 'drip' a continuous infusion into a vein or by a tablet or capsule. A course of chemotherapy may last several weeks. Depending on the cancer, it is more or less likely to produce a remission (temporary or permanent cure). It's common to feel tired for a very variable amount of time after a treatment. There may be other side effects depending on the drug.

  b) Radiotherapy. This works by delivering high-energy particles to the area where cancer cells are growing. The radiation prevents the rapidly dividing cancer cells from reproducing but is much less harmful to normal cells. It is usually administered by using a machine that beams radiation into the affected part of the body. It is given in hospital over a period of several weeks, but you can usually go home after each treatment. Side effects of radiotherapy include soreness of the skin, feeling tired, hair loss, nausea, loss of appetite and diarrhoea.

c) Surgery. This can be undertaken just for investigation as when a biopsy is taken or when the abdomen is opened so that the organs can be directly examined (laparotomy). Alternatively, surgery can aim to remove all or most of the cancerous tissue.

These treatments of cancer can be curative or produce a remission or temporary improvement which may last months or years.

- Treatments for infection. The mainstay of the treatment of infections is antibiotic medication. This is highly or partially effective against bacteria and partially or completely ineffective against viruses. Over the last seventy-five years since they were first used, strains of bacteria that are resistant to antibiotics have developed This means that so-called first-line antibiotics may need to be supplemented with more recently developed second-line antibiotics.

Alternative interventions

These are interventions that do not form part of so-called conventional approaches to treatment as delivered by today's medical practitioners. (They may be by tomorrow's doctors!) All the same, a number of doctors do use them alongside conventional methods. Some, such as acupuncture and hypnosis, have been subjected to rigorous scientific evaluation with uncertain results. Others, such as most herbal remedies, have not been evaluated in this way. The use of some psychological approaches, such as meditation, is often welcomed by doctors who see them as helpful when combined with conventional interventions. If alternative approaches are used by practitioners who strongly believe in them, they are likely to produce positive effects on symptoms at least to begin with. These positive effects may not last and, indeed, may be followed by feelings of disappointment or even depression when it is clear they are not going to produce a lasting effect.

Holistic medicine

These days all doctors claim they take a holistic approach to their patients. By this they mean they take into account the social circumstances in which their patients are living, and psychological as well as physical factors. They see patients and their illnesses as influenced by the setting in which they live. They take an active interest in the relationships patients have with family members and friends as well as in their work or occupations. They try to understand the way their patients react to illness by knowing more about their backgrounds, personalities and previous illness experiences. A doctor may not just take these factors into account, but try to effect changes for the better, for example by trying to increase a patient's social contacts. The term *nidotherapy* (from the Latin, *nidus*, a nest) has been coined to describe attempts to improve the social setting in which patients live.

Unfortunately, although all doctors say they take a holistic approach, because of lack of time or appropriate training or personality or other factors, many do concentrate entirely on the physical aspects of their patients' illnesses. It is then up to family members, friends and patients themselves to think how ways can be found to improve these highly important influences on how patients, even those who are seriously ill, think about themselves.

Symptoms in terminal illnesses

<u>Pain</u> arises for a variety of reasons. (from ischaemia or lack of blood supply, swelling, obstruction, joint problems),

What causes pain? Pain is experienced when the pain receptors are stimulated. They are situated in the skin, muscles and joints as well as in the lining of most bodily organs. These receptors send messages via the sensory nerves back to the brain. The main function of the pain system is to call attention to the fact that all is not well in the part of the body from which the pain arises so that action can be taken to relieve it.

Unfortunately, the causes of pain may not be amenable to change so that symptomatic measures such as pain-relieving drugs or psychological approaches to pain relief need to be used (see below).

Pain in the chest

When the heart or arteries fail to deliver oxygenated blood to a part of the body, the tissue in that part of the body dies. It can't survive without oxygen. The diffuse chest pain, often described as a feeling of heaviness, that occurs with a heart attack is caused by the death of heart muscle which has been deprived of oxygen. When chest pain occurs during exercise, so-called angina, the pain arises from the death of a tiny part of heart muscle. As you age, the blood in a blood vessel serving the heart may clot. If this happens the heart muscle served by that blood vessel will become starved of blood and die. The heart muscle that dies is called ischaemic, and the disease is called ischaemic heart disease. Heart muscle that is in the process of dying gives rise to characteristic, heaviness pain. This is what happens in a 'heart attack'. The surviving heart muscle is often able to carry on supplying the body with oxygen but if, after treatment (see below) there isn't enough such muscle, then heart failure and death will follow.

- Treatments for heart disease
  - a) Drugs. If the heart pump starts to fail, then drugs that stimulate heart muscle may be prescribed. Drugs (diuretics) can also be given

to remove excess water from the body that has accumulated because of heart failure. Finally, drugs can be used to treat abnormalities of heart rhythm such as atrial fibrillation, an irregularity of the heartbeat.

b) Stents. These are small, expandable mesh coils put into arteries to keep them open.

c) Bypass surgery may be performed when one or more of the arteries supplying blood to the heart is blocked. The surgeon uses a graft taken from another artery in the body to create another channel through which blood can flow. Depending on how many arteries are blocked this may involve a double or triple bypass. These operations are now commonly performed by so-called 'keyhole surgery'. Heart transplants are not performed in terminally ill people.

There are many other, more common causes of pain in the chest than heart disease. Fractures of a rib or several ribs as a result of a fall, may cause acute pain. Less acute is the pain caused by a pulled muscle. Lung infections such as bronchitis or pneumonia may also give rise to pain in the chest. Whether the pain is made worse by coughing is a helpful guide to the cause of the pain.

Pain in the abdomen (stomach or belly)

A common cause of acute abdominal pain, often colicky or spasmodic, is an intestinal (gut) infection caused by eating contaminated food or drink. This type of pain is usually accompanied by diarrhoea or vomiting. Colicky pain can also be caused by an obstruction in the intestine, that may be a result of a cancer. If you have an obstruction, this will mean your motions will no longer be able to pass down the gut and you will not be able to pass them.

Chronic abdominal pain occurs with inflammation of part of the intestine. This can be a symptom of cancer or of ulcerative colitis or regional ileitis (also known as Crohn's Disease).

Pain in the back

Most commonly this arises from pressure on one of the nerves emerging from the vertebrae (back bones). As you get older, you are more likely to have some degree of degeneration (osteo-arthritis) of these bones, with narrowing of the inter-vertebral spaces. Pain then occurs along the nerve pathway. This may stretch down into the thigh causing so-called sciatic pain. Thus, much pain in the upper leg is caused by osteo-arthritis of the back bones, though the hip joint may also be osteo-arthritic.

Pain in the back can also be caused by cancer having spread to the bones from another site. Only rarely are bones the site of primary cancers but this does occur.

Pain in other joints

Any joint, especially shoulders, elbows, hand and wrist joints, can be affected by osteo-arthritis. Rheumatoid arthritis is another, less common form of arthritis, most likely to affect the joints in your hands and feet. This form of arthritis is characterised by flare-ups with inflammation of the affected joints and a general feeling of unwellness.

Neurological or neuropathic pain

This occurs as a result of damage to nerves. This may happen as a result of injury or a variety of conditions such as multiple sclerosis.

Treatment of pain

Pain during terminal illness is not the most common but is the most feared symptom. It is generally controllable given effective management. The first step in pain management is to identify the cause of the pain and get that treated. Thus, for example, cardiac or heart pain needs investigation so that there can be an appropriate intervention such as a stent. For some conditions, however, it just is not possible to deal with the cause and treatment is symptomatic.

Although medication is the mainstay of treatment of pain where removal of the cause is not possible, as a preliminary, attention to your mental health is essential if the medication is to work effectively. If you are anxious, frightened or depressed, the pain is much more likely to persist. Talking to someone about your feelings to a sympathetic listener, perhaps a family member or someone in the primary health care team will nearly always be helpful in reducing the experience of pain.

Mild pain responds well to six-hourly paracetamol or a non-steroid anti-inflammatory drug such as ibuprofen. More severe pain generally responds to weak opioids such as codein. The most severe pain is relieved by oral morphine. If this is not helpful, your doctor can prescribe morphine in a different form or try you on a different painkiller. People often worry that, once they start on morphine, they will become addicted to it, but this is not a realistic fear if you have a terminal illness. Further, once you are pain-free, it is sensible to take your pain-killing medication as soon as the pain starts to kick in again. If you allow the pain to build up, it will be more difficult to control. Opioids, such as codeine and morphine do have side-effects. These include headache, constipation, nausea and confusion. These can generally be avoided by adjusting the dose, and taking a laxative and anti-sickness medication as prevention. Constipation is more likely in the bed-bound.

The experience of chronic pain is always an indication for seeking the advice of a health professional. People suffering from intractable pain that does not respond to treatment (especially likely with neurological pain), may benefit from referral to a specialist pain clinic. There are specific painkillers that are helpful at targeting these symptoms.

*Weakness or paralysis of an arm, leg or
facial muscles*

When the blood supply to a part of the brain temporarily fails, this can result in a so-called transient ischaemic attack (TIA), with usually a short-lived loss of the function that part of the brain performs. Thus, a TIA can produce a temporary loss of speech or the loss of the use of an arm or a leg. If the brain supply fails for a longer period, this causes a 'stroke' with a permanent or semi-permanent loss of function. By convention, loss of function that lasts less than 24 hours is regarded as a TIA and as a stroke if it lasts longer. A TIA has to be taken seriously as it indicates a stroke is more likely in the future and there are various reversible causes which may be identified by a series of investigations.

Weakness of one side of the face may occur as part of a TIA or a stroke, but more commonly it is caused by a so-called Bell's palsy. This arises because of damage not to the brain, but to the nerves supplying the facial muscles. It usually improves without treatment over a period of weeks or months

Tiredness/difficulty sleeping at night

What causes tiredness? All chronic illnesses cause tiredness but for some, tiredness is the most prominent symptom. Anaemia, the reduction of red cells in the blood, results in lack of oxygen supply to the brain and other organs of the body and is the most common example. The symptoms of many illnesses involve unusual amounts of muscular effort. So naturally people struggling to breathe or pass motions because they are constipated will suffer from tiredness.

Most commonly, tiredness arises from lack of sleep at night. Most people sleep less at night as they age, but some sleep more. There isn't a 'correct' amount of sleep. People vary greatly in the amount of sleep that suits them. The acid test of whether you are getting enough sleep at night is whether you feel tired during the day. You may have difficulty getting off to sleep or wake very early in the morning and not be able to get back to sleep.

There are various tips to help with night-time sleeping. Avoiding coffee and tea after lunchtime may be helpful. If you find you are wide awake during the night, then it is probably a good idea to listen to the radio or read. Some people find particular programmes send them off to sleep. A milk drink or a drop of Scotch half an hour or so before you settle down to sleep may be helpful.

There is a general view that people who have difficulty sleeping at night should avoid having a sleep during the day. But a regular sleep or siesta after lunch for an hour or so may have no effect on your ability to sleep at night and help you to feel less tired at other times of the day.

Sleeping tablets may be helpful. Some have relatively short-lived effects while the effects of others are longer-lasting. While you may find the effects of sleeping tablets gradually reduce if you use them regularly, if you have a terminal illness, it is probably not sensible to worry about becoming addicted to them.

Appetite disturbance

Loss of appetite and weight is a common accompaniment of many terminal illnesses, especially cancers. Constipation and depression are sometimes responsible but, more commonly, a general feeling of malaise is linked to a lack of interest in many of the things that used to give pleasure to a terminally ill person, with food and drink as two of these. People should not force themselves to eat when they don't feel like it. Terminally ill people who just can't bring themselves to eat despite being encouraged to do so by desperate carers, are sometimes made to feel failures. In this situation, it is a good idea for carers to present small amounts of a terminally ill person's favourite food on a small plate and to just be accepting and remove it if this doesn't stimulate the appetite.

Breathing problems

Difficulty breathing is a common symptom in terminal illness. Causes include heart failure, asthma, lung cancers and chronic obstructive pulmonary disease (COPD). All of these conditions are made worse by anxiety and sometimes anxiety may be the only reason why someone has difficulty breathing. Discussion with a knowledgeable health professional, especially of the fear of choking, is likely to reduce the level of anxiety.

Medical treatment will vary depending on the cause of the problem. Most people breathe more easily, especially at night, if they are at least slightly propped up with pillows. While in hospital a patient can be given oxygen through a mask, and this can be continued at home.

Loss of bladder control

Incontinence of urine is a common problem in terminal illnesses though often it does not occur until nearly the end of life. It is often felt to be one of the most embarrassing of symptoms. Retaining urine between times when you pass it requires some degree of muscular effort so incontinence may arise as part of general muscle weakness. Alternatively, there may be a specific cause such as, for example in men, an infection of the prostate gland or (in both sexes but more commonly in women) a urinary infection. Symptoms of such infections include fever, cloudy urine, pain in passing urine or blood in the urine, but sometimes urinary infections may be asymptomatic so testing the urine for infection is worthwhile even in the absence of symptoms. Confusion is a common accompaniment of a urinary infection and disappears if the infection is successfully treated. Antibiotics are the mainstay of treatment.

For people whose urinary incontinence persists because either no cause can be found or treating the cause does not sort out the problem, incontinence pads may need to be worn. These will need to be regularly changed. People who lie on wet sheets are particularly liable to develop bed sores so regular changing of sheets and examination of the back and buttocks for early signs of such sores is important. When incontinence pads are proving too difficult, fitting an incontinence bag (in men) or, ultimately, a catheter, may be necessary.

Loss of bowel control

This is generally experienced as even more embarrassing than incontinence of urine. Some informal carers find it too distasteful to deal with. The ready availability of a commode may help to avoid it. It may occur towards the end of life as a result of general muscular weakness. Alternatively, it may arise as a result of constipation. A solid lump may prevent the passage of liquid faeces above it and this can leak round the lump and then prove impossible to retain. This is called 'overflow diarrhoea'.

If the cause is constipation, this can be relieved by laxative medication or, if this doesn't work, by insertion of a suppository. In the absence of evidence of constipation, it may turn out that certain foods or alcohol are producing diarrhoea. The omission of these from the diet and constipating medication can be helpful. Both incontinence of urine and of faeces may give rise to unpleasant smells that can be at least partly removed by rapid removal of incontinence bags or sheets and the use of air fresheners.

Swallowing problems

The medical term, dysphagia, merely means difficulty in eating. This is relatively common in terminal conditions. It may occur after a stroke, or be caused by a neurological problem such as Parkinson's Disease, Alzheimer's or a range of other conditions. Some forms of medication produce dysphagia. Sometimes, even with the best medical care, it may be difficult to establish a cause. Swallowing problems may arise from anxiety and indeed, sometimes the relief of anxiety may be sufficient to produce a cure.

Treatment depends on the underlying cause, but whatever is causing the problem it is important to keep drinking in order to avoid dehydration. The diet may need to be altered so as only to include food that is easy to swallow. Tube feeding is a last resort and should only be used with the patient's consent. Speech therapists can do swallowing assessments and make recommendations on food consistency. The risk of not being able to swallow is choking or aspiration (where the food goes down the windpipe and into the lungs instead of down the gullet into the stomach as it should).

Nausea/vomiting

Feeling sick for no obvious reason is a common symptom of terminal illness. Sometimes there is actual vomiting and, if there is, you should have a bowl by your side all the time. There are several possible causes, including some forms of medication. Feelings of anxiety may also be accompanied by nausea. Varying the diet may result in identifying some foods that bring on the nausea. You may also need to be shielded from smells that make you nauseated.

There are several types of anti-sickness tablets, and these may need to be taken regularly if they are to be effective. Unfortunately, some medication effective against nausea produces drowsiness and confusion and cannot be tolerated for this reason. But alternatives can usually be found.

Falls and fractures

Unfortunately, falling is a not infrequent event during a terminal illness and brings problems of its own. The hip is the most frequent site of a fracture. The immobility that necessarily follows a fracture may result in a person becoming vulnerable to infections such as pneumonia which may then prove fatal. Pathological fractures are said to occur when the broken bone is fragile and liable to break even with only mild trauma, because it is already affected by disease such as osteoporosis or infiltrated by cancerous tissue.

Swelling of the legs

Blockage of the veins occurs when the venous blood clots because it is not moving. This can happen when you stand or sit without moving for a prolonged period as during a long flight. A venous clot in the leg causes a blockage, with fluid accumulating below resulting in swelling. Occasionally a bit of the blood clot (an embolus) breaks off and travels up the veins into the chest and through the heart after which it can cause serious damage to the lungs or brain.

Depression

Most people with terminal illness will feel sad and miserable at least some of the time. Often people experience normal depression when they think they have not made the best of their lives or regret the way they have behaved in difficult situations. This is a normal human reaction. But depression can also be an illness. People who are seriously depressed may show withdrawal from all social interaction, refuse food and lose weight, have irrational ideas of guilt for things they have done in the past. They may have suicidal ideas or even make serious attempts at taking their own lives. Indeed, the rate of suicide is distinctly higher in the terminally ill than it is in the general population.

There is no clear dividing line between normal depressive feelings and depression as an illness. The possibility that someone needs assessment and treatment for depression in its own right always needs consideration when they have suicidal ideas or seem more impaired by their mood than they should be given their physical symptoms. The first line of treatment involves listening. Family members and friends can help just by listening to a terminally ill person's depressive thoughts. If this does not seem sufficient and, as is usually the case, the district nurse or family doctor do not have the time to listen, then the GP will often make a referral to a counsellor or psychotherapist.

The family doctor should also consider prescribing anti-depressant medication. There is good evidence that such medication is effective in the treatment of depression even in the last few weeks and months of life. Anti-depressants cannot be expected to work until at least three weeks after the patient starts taking them. Further, most anti-depressant medication has side-effects, especially dryness of the mouth and constipation. If these side-effects are troublesome, then an alternative anti-depressant can usually be found.

Anxiety

Again, this is a normal human reaction in someone who knows they have only a limited term of life ahead of them. Anxiety can be experienced entirely internally with apparently inescapable worrying or, more commonly, there may be bodily symptoms such as palpitations, butterflies in the stomach, feeling faint or weak at the knees. All of these symptoms can be extremely unpleasant.

As far as the focus of worrying is concerned, this is much more commonly linked to fear of the symptoms that may accompany dying than of death itself. Convinced atheists who do not believe in life after death will not fear what will happen to them after they die but may well be frightened of experiencing intolerable pain or of suffocating in their own secretions. Often such fear arises because of previous experience seeing somebody, perhaps a parent, die without good end of life care. There may also be worrying about the future of one or more people who are financially or emotionally dependent on the terminally ill person. Dying people are often much more worried about people they are leaving behind than they are about themselves. Sometimes, so-called 'free-floating' anxiety occurs in which the symptoms of anxiety are experienced without any focus attached to them.

Making sure that, as far as possible, one's affairs are in order, as described in Chapter 9, is likely to relieve at least some anxiety about the future of those who are left behind. Otherwise, listening to anxious preoccupations is the most effective way to help someone who is anxious. This can be done by family members or friends or both. It is sometimes possible to be completely reassuring about a worry. This is the case for symptom control at the end of life. But there are other worries for which no convincing reassurance can be given. Here, just sharing the worry with the person who is terminally ill may be helpful. If anxiety remains a troublesome symptom, then the GP can refer to a counsellor, psychologist or psychotherapist. Cognitive behavioural approaches to crippling anxiety are often highly effective.

Medication to relieve anxiety alongside psychological treatment can also be helpful. So-called anxiolytic drugs such as diazepam (Valium) if prescribed in a dose that reduces anxiety but does not make the person confused, are worth trying. Diazepam has a deserved reputation for leading to drug dependency or addiction but in a terminally ill person this may not be seen as a meaningful drawback.

The end of life

Towards the end of a terminal illness, there comes a point when both the dying person and those around them, their family members, friends and carers accept that no more active treatment is appropriate and that life is going to end in a few hours, days, or at most three of four weeks. Not infrequently this point is not reached simultaneously by everyone concerned and this can lead to increased distress. But from now on, the health care that is provided is known as 'palliative' and has the aim of relieving symptoms without attempting to deal with the cause of the condition. The term 'palliative care' is used to describe caring for someone who has a terminal illness when interventions to produce a cure or more than a brief remission have failed. It may be delivered at home, in some form of residential setting such as a nursing home, in hospital or in a hospice.

It may be difficult for patients and their families to accept that the time for palliative care has come as this involves acknowledging that a search for cure or long-term remission has reached the end of the road. It may take weeks or months for such acceptance to be forthcoming. Once the time has arrived however, a palliative care approach will allow a much stronger and often more effective focus on the relief of symptoms and keeping the patient comfortable. Although a range of professionals is often involved in the delivery of palliative care (district nurse, general practitioner, hospital consultant, medical consultant in palliative care, occupational therapist, pain control specialist, physiotherapist, counsellor) the backbone of the service is usually provided by the district nurse, who may visit as often as daily, backed up by a palliative care nurse who may visit two or three times a week.

At the very end of life, there are four main symptoms medication aims to control – pain and breathlessness, nausea and vomiting, agitation and secretions it is no longer possible to swallow. Family doctors and palliative care teams are able to advise on medication for these symptoms. It is usual to have a box at home with the injectable medications in it, just in case they are needed at the end of life. It is good to be prepared in advance and plan for what might be needed before that time comes.

With the emphasis now on keeping the dying person comfortable, health care follows the patient's symptoms with the aim of ensuring a smooth transition towards a calm, easy death. If the patient develops a new set of symptoms, for example those of a pneumonia, these are not treated curatively with antibiotics, for this would only unnecessarily prolong suffering. When nearing the very end of life, the family doctor may want to discuss stopping some medications and starting others. It may no longer be possible, for example, to swallow whole tablets and some medication may be changed to a liquid form. When swallowing even small amounts of liquid is no longer an option, medication can be given by skin patch or an injection. If injections are needed more than a few times, medication can be put into a syringe with a tiny needle under the skin so that it can be given continuously. This involves using a gadget called a syringe driver. Whether in hospital, hospice or at home, the nursing team manage injectable medication.

This is the point at which members of the family will want to come and say their goodbyes. The dying patient who remains conscious will greatly value the opportunity for a few last words with their close family and friends, perhaps sharing memories as well as thoughts for the future. The presence of others will, in itself, reduce the anxiety of the dying person. It is at this point that religious people may ask to see a priest, whose visit may also be a calming influence. There may come a point when the dying person is too tired to see more people and this, of course, should be respected. Not infrequently, when the person finally stops eating and drinking completely, there may be a period of agitated distress. Usually, this only lasts for a short time, but if it persists, then it can be helped with morphine, perhaps delivered by a syringe driver.

As the final illness reaches its end, with failure of the liver and kidneys, there is an accumulation in the blood of toxins which cloud the mind and induce drowsiness. The patient will spend longer and longer periods asleep and will finally lapse into a permanent coma before the last breath is taken. During the last hour or two, the patient may make noises in the throat, the so-called 'death rattle', which sound distressing though, in reality, the dying person is beyond the experience of distress. Even after the patient has taken what was apparently a last breath, for a few minutes, every twenty or thirty seconds, patients may take further breaths (this is called Cheyne-Stokes breathing), until finally they breathe no more.

This is a time when those in the room may experience intense emotion, perhaps a sense of relief that the dying person's suffering has at last ended, mixed with intense grief at the finality of such a loss. For some time after the last breath, those in the room, family, friends, carers, may have a sense that the person who has died is still in the room. This sensation may last for some hours before it too finally fades.

CHAPTER 4

The Helping Services

Readers with a health background will probably wish to skip all or most of this chapter as it is unlikely to contain information which they do not already know.

Introduction

What follows is a description of the current pattern of services in the UK at the time of writing (mid-2023). At this point in time, all services are under extreme pressure, especially as a result of inadequate numbers of staff at every level. This has been caused by a combination of Covid, Brexit, strikes, inadequate numbers of doctors and nurses, the war in the Ukraine with consequent severe financial pressures. For whatever reasons, the result is that, in many places, the NHS has long waiting lists for all types of services and sometimes the service provided is nowhere near as good as it has been in the past.

There are, broadly speaking, two types of services (health and social services), employed by two different bodies (the NHS and local authorities), whose job it is to help people who are terminally ill and those caring for them. As you will see, the system is complicated, indeed unnecessarily complicated. The two types of service are supposed to work closely together and often they do, but most authorities agree it would be better if these two systems were completely fused. Successive governments have failed to achieve such integration.

SUMMARY OF THE STRUCTURE OF THE HELPING SERVICES

NHS Services

The Primary Health Care Team

This may include GPs, nurses, specialist nurses, physiotherapists, occupational therapists, pharmacists, social workers, counsellors and sometimes others.

NHS 111

111 is the emergency number if you have an urgent medical problem. It is largely staffed by nurses.

This service can also be accessed online by going to 111.nhs.uk

The Community Health Services

These include community or district nurses, specialist nurses, specialist doctors (who may have regular sessions in primary health care premises), palliative care, community palliative care and some other services such as podiatry and wheelchair services. They also provide equipment for the home, often at very short notice, such as a hospital bed, commode, toilet raise.

Hospitals (see below)

Hospices (see below)

Although hospices are independently run by charitable organisations, on average about 30% of their funding comes from the NHS.

Social Services

These services provide social care. This covers a wide range of activities. It includes support in people's own homes (home or domiciliary care), for example with washing and dressing and getting out of bed in the morning. Social services also provide day centres as well as residential care in care homes and nursing homes.

Community social workers are the gatekeepers for these types of social care. They carry out assessments to find out what type of care and support a person needs and offer information and counselling regarding, for example, the financial benefits to which people in need are entitled.

NHS Services

The Primary Health Care Team

The days when the family doctor or GP (general practitioner) was virtually the only source of medical help in the community (primary health care) are long over. Nowadays primary health care is provided by a range of health professionals of which the GP is only one. All the same, the service is usually based in one building, though there is now a much larger number of people working in it. These include:

Reception staff. These are the gatekeepers to the rest of the staff. They are supervised by a practice manager. You can contact the practice either online, using an e-consult form or by phone. If you phone, you will first hear a long message encouraging you to use the e-consult form, to be polite to the reception staff (very necessary as you may well feel so irritated with the system you will be tempted to be rude), and with various other pieces of information. You will then be told how long you will have to wait to speak to a member of the reception staff. It is as well to put the phone on speaker and have a book to read or something else to get on with, while you wait. The member of the reception staff who answers will want to know why you are calling. They will then usually offer a phone or face to face appointment, usually with a doctor or a practice nurse. Although you will have a named GP, it is quite likely that an appointment will be offered for someone who is not your named doctor.

General practitioner. These may be partners in the practice or salaried doctors. Medical partners, as well as carrying out their medical role seeing patients, are responsible, together with the practice manager, for the administration and have a financial stake in the practice. As well as partners and salaried doctors, you may be seen by a trainee general practitioner, who is supervised by a more experienced doctor. Your GP is likely to be the person who coordinates your care. Hopefully this doctor will already have known you for several years before you reach this final stage. They are likely to be in communication with the hospital team and to be responsible for referring you to the palliative care and community nursing team. Together, these provide in-depth support for patients with chronic illnesses, such as asthma, diabetes and hypertension.

Practice nurses. These have a variety of roles. They work in teams, providing a wide range of tasks including dressings, blood tests, ECGs and a range of support. The practice is also likely to employ specialist nurses, including a diabetic nurse and one or more community psychiatric nurses.

Other professionals. These may include physiotherapists, occupational therapists, pharmacists, social workers and counsellors.

NHS 111 Emergency Service

This is the number to ring if you have an urgent medical problem and your general practice is closed because it is out of hours or for some other reason. The adviser, usually a nurse, will ask you questions about your problem and then either just give you advice or get you a face to face or phone appointment with someone at your general practice or advise you to go to an Accident and Emergency Department or tell you how to get any medicine you need. If you are struggling to get through to your practice, this is a good way of getting help.

The Community Health Services

Community nurses. For people with terminal illnesses, community nurses (previously and sometimes still known as district nurses) are the health professionals who are most likely to provide most of your care. Your first contact with a community nurse is likely to be with a senior nurse who will make a *care plan* for you which will describe your needs and how these are to be met. A copy of this plan will be left with you. Members of the community nursing team will then provide this care as well as mobilising other community resources, including those provided by voluntary organisations such as the Macmillan nursing team for people with cancer. They also act as a link with hospital services.

Palliative care nurses. These will care for you at the very end of your life. They may be employed by the community health service or provided as an outreach service by your local hospice. There are two types of nurses. One is highly specialist and is based at the hospice and has access to the palliative care specialist doctors. They have a wealth of experience managing patients nearing the end of their lives. The other is a team of nurses, sometimes provided by the hospice and sometime by the social services or a voluntary sector organisation such as Marie Curie, who care for patients nearing the end of their lives. The hospice team includes a number of other professionals such as psychologists, holistic therapists and social workers.

Physiotherapists. A community physiotherapist will assess your needs for physiotherapy, especially exercises and then arrange for this to be provided.

Occupational therapists. These will visit you at home and make an assessment of any aids or equipment you may need or any alterations to your accommodation that might be necessary. These might include grab rails and a chair for your shower, rails or a stair lift for your stairs, a wheelchair or walking frame to help you get around.

Hospitals

Most hospitals in the UK are run by the National Health Service (NHS) and are free. A small number are independent and run for profit. Most NHS hospitals are general and contain both out-patient clinics and in-patient services. There is a small number of specialist hospitals, especially in London, dealing only, for example, with cancer, cardiology or mental illness. Some hospitals are affiliated with academic centres or medical schools.

Out-Patient Services

Most general hospitals run out-patient clinics for all the medical specialties. Oncology (cancer), cardiology (heart), chest (lung) and geriatric (elderly) clinics are the specialities most likely to be seeing terminally ill patients. There are waiting lists for all services, but these are not supposed to be longer than two weeks for cancer patients and eighteen weeks for other patients.

Attendance at an out-patient clinic generally follows a referral from your GP.

In-Patient Services

Admission to hospital often occurs following an assessment by your GP who arranges a bed, so you do not have to go via the Accident and Emergency Department and wait outside in an ambulance. However sometimes admission does occur from the A and E department or following referral from an out-patient department.

Patients admitted as in-patients used to be under the care of a particular, named consultant but are now more likely to be the responsibility of a team of consultants so you may not see the same consultant twice. Consultants are fully trained doctors, usually with experience in a particular specialty. They nearly all have doctors in training attached to them and supervised by them. Often these training doctors are the ones you mainly see. Your junior doctor may be in his or her first year after qualification (Foundation Training) or be in Year 2 of such training (FY2). They then proceed to

Junior and then Senior Middle Grade posts until they are appointed to consultant positions after about eight years. Towards the end of their training, these so-called junior doctors are very experienced.

Hospices

In general, hospices have only a small number of beds. Nowadays, most have outreach services, providing specialist palliative care services who can visit the home and give advice over the phone. The services hospices provide are reserved for patients who require the expertise of specialists in end-of-life care. Admission to a hospice does not necessarily mean, however, that, once admitted, patients remain there until death. Some hospices admit patients with terminal illnesses when they are very ill, but then discharge them once they are well enough to go home until such time as they need admission again. Usually, you are admitted when you have symptoms that need the expertise of the hospice team. Further, hospices will often admit patients with terminal illness for a week or two for respite to give their carers a break. As the end of life approaches, most have a policy of allowing family members the right to visit patients at any time of the day or night.

Privately funded health care

Almost all health services, including hospice care, are obtainable through the private sector. Especially in

London but also in other major cities, private health care is readily available. It is extremely expensive and most people who use it have taken out or had taken out for them private health insurance. Many senior executives have private health care insurance as part of their package of benefits. Although there is a small number of doctors who only work privately, most private care is delivered by doctors who also work for the NHS.

The main advantages of private care are the much shorter waiting lists, the assurance that the person delivering the care, for example an operation, will be a named consultant and the privacy of a room to yourself. However, for various reasons, many people who have taken our private health insurance prefer to use the NHS. This is particularly the case for medical emergencies and for those with specialist nursing needs which may not be readily available on private wards.

Social Services

If you have any social care needs, including help with washing, dressing, feeding or toileting, then you will need to be in contact with a social worker from your local Social Services Department. A social worker will then visit you to assess your needs and work out how these can be met. Alternatively, if you have been in hospital, a hospital social worker will alert your local Social Service Department before your discharge to arrange for your social care needs to be met as soon as you leave hospital. It is also useful for you to know the telephone number of your local social services helpline. You can find this on the Council website or your GP or community nurse will give it to you.

If you need it, a member or more than one member of the Social Service care team will visit you one or more times a day to wash and dress you and help you with your toilet needs. This service may be contracted out to a private company. You are entitled to this service free for up to six weeks after leaving hospital after which you will have to pay for it. You may also be eligible for having meals delivered to you in your home (meals on wheels) if you are living alone and can no longer cook.

Day Care Centres. These are thin on the ground, but when they exist are generally run by private companies or, occasionally by voluntary organisations, though they are paid for by local authorities or privately by individuals using them. They generally run five days a week, but patients may only attend for part of the week. They provide a range of clinical and social services as well as a variety of activities depending on the client group. Some do not admit patients with dementia; others only admit such patients, but most are mixed.

Residential Care Homes. These provide care for people who can no longer live at home. Most commonly this is because they have some degree of dementia and do not have family members who can look after them. They are now nearly all run for profit by private companies though some residents receive financial support from their local authorities. Such authorities fully support people whose total assets do not exceed £23,250. All residents with greater assets than this, have to make a financial contribution to their care. Many (about a third) are fully self-funded and pay the entire cost of their care.

Residential Nursing Homes. These are for people who cannot be looked after at home and, in addition, require nursing care. These homes are also run by private companies with most residents financially supported wholly or in part by local authorities. They have a higher ratio of trained nurses and a higher level of medical care than residential care homes.

Financial benefits to which you may be entitled

Terminally ill people may have savings or investments in the form of stocks and shares, bonds, bank deposits etc. Most will have some form of occupational pension. In addition, all men and women over the age of 66, depending on their National Insurance Record, are entitled to the statutory state pension. The retirement age will go up in 2026.

- Attendance allowance is for people over state pension age who have a disability severe enough to need someone to look after them either by day or by night. They must have needed help for at least 6 months or be terminally ill. The rate is higher if you need help both by day and by night. The benefit is stopped if you are in a care home paid for by the Local Authority. It is not means tested.

- Carer's Allowance. This is payable to carers who spend more than 35 hours a week caring alone for someone who is receiving attendance allowance. This is not means tested but is taxable.

- NHS continuing healthcare. You may qualify for free social care arranged and funded solely by the NHS if you have long-term complex health needs. Before qualifying for this benefit, which may be of considerable value but has a high bar, you will need to be assessed by a multi-disciplinary NHS team. To be eligible, they will need to find that you have a priority need in at least two areas of disability. Accessing this is usually initiated by the community nursing team or hospital team by contacting social services. However, if you think you may be entitled to this benefit, you should raise this with your community nurse or social worker.

Privately funded home care

Local authority funded home care is limited to a maximum of six weeks after discharge from hospital. It is quite likely that people with terminal illnesses will, if they can afford it, wish to employ home carers. Their needs may range from someone coming in to clean for a couple of hours once a week to whole time seven days a week, twenty four hour care. The best way to identify home carers is by personal recommendation from other members of your family or from friends. If this does not work, then you may be able to find carers by looking at advertisements in your local newspaper or newsagent. There you will also find advertisements for companies that provide such care. The advantage of companies, which are generally more expensive than if you make private arrangements, is that they provide cover for holidays, sickness or unexpected absences.

CHAPTER 5

Description of the interview with a family member

I carried out personal interviews with a surviving family member of twenty-three out of the twenty-four of our friends who had died over recent years. These interviews were all carried out between November 2021 and September 2022. In most cases the interviewee was the surviving partner but in a few it was a child of our late friend. One was with a niece. These were all with people I knew at least reasonably well and indeed I had been in touch with most of them, sometimes quite frequently, in the last few months of the life of the terminally ill person and subsequently. All the same, in nearly all the interviews I learned much that I had not known previously. One interview was held on Zoom but the others were all face to face.

I began by explaining the main purpose of the interview which was to gain information about ways in which the quality of life of terminally ill people could be improved. By definition, the ultimate outcome of a terminal illness was death, but I knew enough to know that, at least sometimes, there were ways in which things might have gone better. I was asking for help to add to my existing knowledge. There were other purposes to the interview, including a description of ways of behaving or interventions that had been helpful. Finally, I wanted to know more about what difference, if any, the presence or absence of religious faith made to the experience of terminal illness. I explained that I knew we would be going over painful memories and that if, at any time, my interviewee wished to put a stop to the interview, they should say so.

The format was that of a semi-structured interview of which I had experience going back over nearly sixty years. I began by asking my interviewee to describe the last few months or years of the terminally ill person's life, mentioning particularly anything that seemed relevant to the purpose of the interview. I encouraged the interviewee to go on talking without interruption for as long as they wanted. Then, when they had finished this spontaneous account, I went on to ask questions to fill in gaps. I had prepared a series of questions in my mind (written down on a sheet in front of me), so that, by the end of the interview, I knew that I would have the answers to a series of relevant questions.

This meant that, by the end of the interview, which usually lasted between an hour and a quarter to an hour and a half, I had been given an account of the last few months or years since the terminal illness began, the point at which it became clear that recovery was not going to occur, the length of any period of dependency, what sort of communication there had been about dying and death with the terminally ill person, the quality of communication with health professionals, and how things might have gone differently or better. I also asked about the religious views of both my interviewee and the terminally ill person. If, as was nearly always the case, there was a lack of belief in an afterlife, I asked what difference, if any, this lack of belief had made.

The day after the interview I wrote to the family member thanking them for their help and apologising for any distress I might have caused. In a number of cases, the interviewee wrote back saying that in fact the interview had been helpful in clarifying their memories and feelings about this period in their lives. This was less likely to happen if the interviewee had already spent some time talking to someone, a bereavement counsellor or a therapist, about their experience. All in all, though, I felt the interview had served some sort of positive function.

CHAPTER 6

Improving the quality of the end of life: Lessons from the interviews

This and the following chapter are based largely on what I learned from the interviews I held with family members of my friends who had died. A quarter, or six of our friends, a slightly higher than expected rate, died in a state of advanced dementia. The interviews held with these family members were dominated by the problems brought about by their lack of understanding that their days were numbered. This meant meaningful communication was extremely difficult or impossible. For this reason, I've devoted the next chapter to the final months of those of our friends with dementia.

What is a good quality of life at the end of life?

In my interviews with family members of our friends who had died, my main aim was to find out how they thought the quality of life could be improved during their terminal illnesses. In other words, to what degree was my terminally ill friend given the best opportunity to 'go gentle' or at least, to go as gentle as possible.

In only two of the interviews did the family members claim that the end of life of the person who had died could not have been better. As it happens, in both cases, these were adult children talking about the deaths of their father and mother. In both cases, their two parents had had terminal illnesses that were strikingly different one from another in the degree of distress experienced both by the dying person and by those around them.

The last illness, described by her son, of a French friend living in Paris was deeply distressing both to herself and to her family. About five years before she died in 2017, she began to lose her memory. Over the next three years, she gradually moved from just being unable to remember where she had put things to failing to recognise even her own children and grandchildren. For the last two years of her life, she was severely disabled by her dementia. Even more painful than her cognitive decline was a change in personality. She had always been somewhat impatient and prone to irritability but now she became aggressive, occasionally, given the chance, physically attacking those around her even including the family members of whom she had been so fond. This meant that while she was awake, she had to have somebody with her to restrain her if she became hostile. Eventually, when her Alzheimer's Disease was advanced, she was admitted to hospital with 'flu, from which she died.

The last months of her husband, who died five months later, were in great contrast. Although he had developed tuberculosis during his National Service in the French army in Algeria, he was in relatively good health until about four years before he died when he began to suffer with tiredness and lack of energy. He was diagnosed with an unusual form of leukaemia but was kept alive with medication and blood transfusions. When his wife, who had needed an enormous amount of care from him, died, he lost all motivation to continue living and soon died. His last months were relatively tranquil as he had accepted he was shortly going to die and felt his time had come. His son was able to talk to his father about his impending death the day before he died. According to his son, his father was both a little scared and quite relieved as he did not want to live longer. This does not mean that his son took the deaths of his parents lightly. On the contrary, their deaths hit him hard. 'You can't make an abstraction of death', he repeated more than once, 'It's for real.' His son put what he called the 'good deaths' of his parents down to strong family support, the excellent quality of the carers whom the family was able to afford financially, good medical care and a very high level of communication between members of the family who were in contact daily.

The other deaths that their sons said 'could not have been better' were described by their sons, again of their parents. Their father developed a cancer of the mouth about eighteen months before he died. Despite active treatment, the cancer gradually spread which meant not only that he could not swallow and had to be fed by tube, but it became increasingly difficult for him to speak clearly and make himself understood. All his teeth had to be extracted before he could have radiotherapy. He suffered quite severe pain in his mouth though it was possible to control this reasonably well with medication. All the same, he was restless at night and slept poorly. He fell out of bed a number of times and this posed major problems as he was too heavy for his wife to get him back into bed. Calling the ambulance to help lift him posed problems as the paramedics, following instructions, put pressure on his wife to have her husband admitted to hospital which neither of them wanted. Eventually, the husband became too disabled to manage at home and he was admitted to a local hospice where he died five days after admission. This last admission was distressing as he was sometimes confused and often shouted saying he wanted to go home.

His wife survived him by just over six years. About five months before she died, she complained of just 'not feeling right' and was rapidly diagnosed with a cholangiocarcinoma, a rare form of cancer of the bile duct. An extensive operation can be performed for this condition. but it has only modest success and involves an extremely distressing post-operative period. She was offered this operation but opted not to have it, a decision with which her doctors agreed. She was given excellent palliative care and gradually lost weight and energy until she was admitted to the same local hospice as her husband had been. She was lucid until virtually the end and died peacefully, as she had wished, with her family around her.

In some ways, while it is understandable that their children should regard the husband of the French couple and the wife of the other couple as having had 'good deaths', it seems extraordinary that they should think the same about the wife of the French couple and the other husband. During my conversations with them, it transpired that when they described deaths as 'good', the children meant that, given the nature of their illnesses, the latter had had as good deaths as possible. The medical and nursing care had been, in their view, excellent. The doctors had communicated well. The family had been able to provide a high level of emotional support and had been able to afford good social care.

An important lesson which can be learned from the experience of these two families is that we need to judge the quality of life separately from the quality of care. Some types of terminal illness are inevitably accompanied by a great deal of physical and/or emotional distress. In other cases, the last round of cards one is dealt means it is possible for one's final months, weeks and days before death to be relatively free of physical or emotional pain. Of course, the nature of the terminal illness is only one element to be considered in judging the quality of a death. The end of a human existence, a final parting with family and friends, these are momentous occasions no matter to what extent they have been predicted. But in considering how the quality of life can best be maintained in the last phase of life, the symptoms produced by the terminal illness are a most important consideration.

There was one very significant difference between these two couples in their attitudes towards their illnesses. The English couple were both practising Christians with a strong belief in the existence of a deity, though not, as it happens, in an afterlife. They saw their illnesses in the light of their Christian faith. The Parisian couple were secular Jews who were both confirmed atheists. In terms of the quality of life of the two couples during their terminal illnesses, this seemed to make no difference, except possibly in the last two or three days of life. At this point, both members of the Christian couple appeared to be much helped by conversations with their priest. Their sons both thought this was a positive element in their last few days. The French wife's level of understanding was not such that she would, in any case, have appreciated a conversation of this type. While her husband's last two or three days were calm and he showed no signs of agitation, he did not have the positive experience enjoyed by the Christian couple. This raises the question whether for atheists in their last few days of life, there might be a case for offering the opportunity of a conversation with a counsellor. Of course, most might well reject this idea, not wanting to talk to a relative stranger at this time of their lives. The priest with whom the Christian couple conversed in their last few days was someone who had been known to them for some years and this was surely an undoubted advantage.

The last months and years of these two couples illustrate how, even with superb health care, it is not possible for some terminally ill people to 'go gentle'. All that can be achieved is that they go as gently as possible. With most terminally ill people, a dignified end, relatively free of distress, is well within the bounds of possibility. The remainder of this chapter aims to provide some pointers how this can best be achieved.

How to improve health care

1. How to avoid a delay in diagnosis

Delay can occur for a variety of reasons. My friend with cancer of the tongue described above was on holiday in Devon when he had some pain in his mouth. He went to a local dentist who found a suspicious lump. The dentist wrote to his general practitioner but for some reason there was a bureaucratic delay and an appointment from an oncology clinic was not sent for three months during which time almost certainly the cancer had spread and become more difficult to treat.

For two years before he died in July 2012, one of my friends who was a hardy swimmer and who, all his life, had loved nothing more than a dip in the freezing North Sea, decided he didn't enjoy it anymore. He became breathless with exercise, consulted the family doctor but delayed having the recommended blood test for a few weeks until after his eightieth birthday celebrations, fearing he might have to go into hospital. He was referred by his general practitioner to the local hospital. There he was investigated but unfortunately, although there was an abnormality in a scan of his abdomen carried out in February 2010, the significance of this finding was not appreciated until nine months later when he was admitted to hospital. It is not clear if these delays affected the outcome, but certainly his disease was more advanced than it need have been before treatment began.

The NHS has rules about wait times when there is a serious suspicion a patient might have cancer. Hospital doctors are expected to respond within two weeks to a referral from a GP when there is this possibility. Further, patients are expected to have a diagnosis within twenty-eight days. Anyone who thinks they might have cancer should therefore press hard for a GP appointment leading to a hospital referral. When it came to his own needs, my friend with a cancer of the tongue, in line with his personality, was self-effacing and reluctant to push for an earlier appointment. In general, if there is the possibility of a cancer diagnosis, the longer one waits, the more time-consuming one's care will be.

There is a difficult balance to be struck here. Early diagnosis is indeed important in the case of cancers, but family doctors would be overwhelmed if their patients insisted on a rapid appointment for every minor symptom that might, just possibly, indicate a cancer. It is however perfectly reasonable to press for urgent diagnosis in the presence of a symptom such as a suspicious lump that is specific for a particular cancer.

How to achieve continuity of medical and nursing care

One of my friends suffered over a period of sixteen years from a slowly progressive neurological disorder. This was initially diagnosed as Parkinson's disease, but this diagnosis was later revised to a related condition - supranuclear bulbar palsy. Over the whole of this period, his primary care was delivered by the same general practitioner. She only worked two or three sessions a week so, in an emergency, it was necessary for other doctors to be involved. But the continuity of care she provided was an important element in his care. It meant that his wife always felt there was someone knowledgeable who really knew her and her husband that she could turn to.

In contrast, another of my friends suffered from a rare form of blood clotting disorder, diagnosed about two years before he died in January 2017. His condition required highly specialist hospital care, but he also had need for attention from his general practice. His wife found it extremely difficult to speak to any doctor in the practice, let alone the GP with whom he was signed up. She had to negotiate with an aggressive receptionist explaining precisely what the problem was, before she had any hope of a medical consultation. In the last two months of his life, he needed home visits which were provided by a series of different, young and clearly inexperienced doctors who spent most of the time they had available reading the notes to bring themselves up to date. About a month before he died, an older, more experienced family doctor visited the home. He came down to the living room after seeing my friend and told the assembled family members to sit down so that he could talk to all of them. He then explained in bald terms that their husband/father was dying and had only a few weeks, perhaps days to live. He would call the local palliative care team. According to his wife, the family had no idea things were as bad as this. Her husband did indeed die two or three weeks later. The lack of continuity previously had meant that doctors meeting the family for the first time had been unable to bring themselves to talk in an open and honest way with the family.

Continuity of care is perhaps the single most important aspect of primary care influencing the quality of care of a terminal illness. If primary care professionals have to consult notes or take a fresh history every time they are consulted, they are unlikely to be able to provide a satisfactory service. At the moment, only a minority of general practices make a point of trying to provide continuity of care. This is sometimes not easy because so many family doctors work part-time, but a 'buddy' system which works so that only two doctors are involved with each patient, achieves a high level of continuity. Patients and the relatives of patients can sometimes learn how to achieve continuity of care for themselves by understanding better the system of appointments of their own practice. It may be necessary to wait a few extra days to see the doctor you want but this may be well worthwhile. You may be able to learn only to call the practice when your preferred doctor is on duty for emergencies and, if you ask, reception may tell you when this is the case. Achieving as much continuity of care is important as you are more likely to trust a doctor who knows you and conversely, a doctor will be more open with someone he or she has been in touch with before. The patients in general practices that achieve a high level of continuity have better health care outcomes including, so a Norwegian study showed, a lower death rate.

2. *How to achieve good communication with health professionals*

Among our friends, there were some who felt that the communication with their doctors and other health professionals was excellent. One of the reasons that the son of our late French friends thought the quality of life of his parents during their terminal illnesses could not have been better was because the Parisian doctors who looked after them explained the illnesses and their treatments to the best of their understanding, gave them their best estimate of how long there was to go and spent as much time as was necessary to go through all aspects of their conditions. The sons of the English couple also described above, talked about a session they had with the multidisciplinary team looking after their mother, which went on for the best part of an hour so that they could explore every aspect of the management of her cancer. The part-time GP of my friend with a neurological disorder always seemed to have time to discuss the numerous problems that arose with his care. The GP of a friend who decided to end his life by voluntarily stop eating and drinking (described in much more detail in a later chapter), was as supportive as he could be within the limits of the law.

With a small number of my friends, important information was withheld from them, either deliberately or inadvertently. For example, one of my friends was diagnosed with a cancer of the prostate some years before he died in October 2021. About two years before he died, he developed unusual seizures that were resistant to anticonvulsant medication. In March 2021, the neurologist looking after this aspect of his care wrote that he needed a scan of his brain as, it was stated in the letter, he was known to have metastases (secondary growths) from his prostate cancer. This was complete news to him and his family as they had previously been told his cancer had not spread. It turned out that a secondary deposit in his bones had been discovered in October 2020, but no one had told them. To make matters worse, the neurologist then left a message on the home answer phone that the diagnosis of epilepsy might be wrong and that perhaps he should be on different medication. Leaving a message with such sensitive information on an answer phone is, of course, quite inappropriate as there is no way of knowing who is going to listen to it. This faulty communication was the subject of a complaint to the hospital management, to which the hospital responded with a partial admission of failure. The failure to communicate the spread of the cancer had meant that neither the patient nor the family were able to plan the future in the light of the reality of the situation.

Further, some family doctors and hospital specialists always seemed to have too little time to discuss the questions that the patient or family members wished to raise. One friend was referred to a urologist who diagnosed a cancer of the prostate and without any discussion told him he was going onto hormone treatment. This was doubtless the best option. but my friend and his wife felt disempowered by the lack of any opportunity to consider alternative courses of action. At a later point in his treatment, he was found to have an abnormal finding on a blood test. The GP who was on call, again without any discussion, told him he would have to go into hospital for critically urgent treatment, not being willing to allow any alternative. Following careful discussions between themselves, my friend and his wife decided to refuse hospital admission and abide by any consequences. In the event, the situation was not critical and hospital admission turned out not to have been needed. In the end it turned out that a hospital admission was unnecessary. Admission might not have been recommended if the GP involved had had previous contact with him.

These were examples of the patient being treated as a passive recipient of medical care rather than as a partner. Generally, patients were treated with respect, but there were one or two examples of situations in which this was not the case. Incredibly, one consultant surgeon, when asked by one of my late friends about the reasons why he had to wait so long for an investigation, said to him: 'Mr. X, as far as I'm concerned, you are a statistic. You are a number on my waiting list.' The dehumanising impact of such a statement needs no emphasis.

In thinking about ways in which patients and their family members can succeed in having good communication with the health professionals it is important to remember that not all people with terminal illness want to hear the truth. There is sometimes a silent conspiracy between patients, family members and doctors to deny the seriousness of an illness and its likely fatal outcome. Doctors are usually well aware when patients and their family members are in denial, and most would not regard it as their job to force a confrontation but rather to move the conversation into as realistic a realm as the patient and family can cope with. However, there are some doctors, particularly the young and inexperienced, but not only those, who shy away from talking about the possibility of dying and either avoid it altogether or delegate a discussion with the family to a junior member of the team. When it was felt by the medical team that there were no more treatment options for one of my friends and that she should be transferred to a hospice or nursing home for the last few weeks of her life, the hospital consultant left it to a young occupational therapist to tell the family to find an alternative placement for her. The attitude of some senior doctors to palliative care is illustrated by the story told me by the son of one of my friends who had died. On applying for entry to medical school, this man, now a senior geriatrician, told the Dean of the medical school to which he was applying that he had spent some time working in a hospice. 'What on earth did you want to do that for?', said the Dean, 'Are you sure you want to be a doctor?', the assumption being that doctors only worked to cure.

But, of course, it is not only doctors who are reluctant to talk about fatal outcomes. One wife found the most distressing part of her husband's protracted and painful final illness was his completely unrealistic insistence until two weeks before he died that things were going to get better and that he and she would be able to travel to places on which he had set his heart, particularly Vienna and Nice. She missed not talking to him about the fact he was dying. He did express some worries about what would happen to her when he eventually died, and she felt she could perhaps have taken the opportunity to talk to him about his death when he raised these concerns. Another friend and his wife never talked about the possibility he might die. The wife felt this is what her husband wanted and, indeed, if they had talked about it, there was nothing additional they would have wanted to say to each other that they did not in fact, say. She insisted he had not wanted to be told more and that his wishes should be respected. This was not a view shared by my friend's brother who rang me three weeks before he died asking if there should not be a conversation with his brother in which he was told he was near death. At the time, I raised this possibility with both my friend's wife and son, but they decided they did not wish to impose any such conversation upon him. This is not what he would have wanted.

Thus, it is clear that what counts as a 'good' conversation with a doctor will vary depending on the hopes and expectations of a patient and family members. For one widowed friend, a 'good' conversation would have been one in which the likely fatal outcome was openly discussed. For her husband, a 'good' conversation would not have included the possibility of death. The result was that no conversation of any kind with a doctor took place. The only conversations which did take place were those that involved the introduction of new forms of treatment, most of which had little hope of changing the outcome. For my friends in denial, a 'good' conversation would not have mentioned death and would have been limited to immediate concerns about symptoms and their treatment.

In contrast, there were a number of our friends who died and their family members who did wish for a full and frank discussion not only about symptoms and treatment but about the likely outcome no matter how depressing this might turn out to be. For this to happen, the patient and family members need to make clear to the doctor that this is what they want. They can do this by reassuring the doctor about their preparedness to hear whatever he or she has to say, by saying things like: 'We know you can't be certain, but we really would like to know your best estimate of the time or at least the range of time he/she has left.' It may be thought it is no part of a patient's job to make the doctor's life easier, but if the doctor patient relationship is seen as a partnership of equals, then it becomes clear why this should indeed be something the patient and family members should aim for.

GPs and hospital specialists should be the first port of call when patients and their family members wish to find out more about their illnesses. They are able to tailor their knowledge to the individual circumstances of the people they are informing, and this is important for the same diagnosis may have very different implications for different people. Nowadays, most people will want to access the internet to find out more about what is wrong with them or their family members. There are many web sites putting out inaccurate or irrelevant information. There are two medical sources that can be trusted. The NHS and Mayo Clinic web sites are well researched. The web sites emanating from patient organisations are highly variable in quality. Some are excellent; others are either unnecessarily alarmist or over-optimistic. One very useful source of information is the Health Experiences web site. This consists of patients with particular diagnoses or conditions talking about their own experiences at different stages of their illnesses.

The surviving relatives of our friends reported very variable levels of satisfaction with their family doctors, hospital consultants and other health professionals during their terminal illnesses. The highest levels of satisfaction were achieved when patients and their family members felt that they were in partnership with the health professionals responsible for care. Partnership was best achieved when health professionals were open about what they knew, and patients and family members were as knowledgeable as they could be about the illnesses from which they were suffering (see Chapter 3 for relevant medical information and for the way to use web sites most effectively).

An important barrier to good communication is the insistence of some terminally ill patients to refuse to allow their close relatives (especially partners and adult children) to accompany then when they attended their family doctors or hospital consultants. When this happened, this meant that family members were often in the dark about what their terminally ill relative had been told as, inevitably, information given by doctors is selectively filtered before it is communicated by the patient. The presence of relatives at the consultation will always mean that more relevant questions are asked, and a better idea is received of proposed treatments and their possible side-effects.

While clearly there are some terminally ill patients and family members for whom open communication about dying is so terrifying it is never going to happen, for most in this situation 'going gentle' will be easier if there is a free flow of information between family members as well as between the family and the members of the health care teams.

Dealing well with symptom control

Measures to control symptoms are discussed at some length in Chapter 3. In what follows here, I've described the impact of symptoms on the quality of life of my friends during their terminal illnesses. Inevitably, there is some overlap and repetition.

Sleep and tiredness

Most of my friends, towards the very end of their lives, lost energy and slept for longer periods of time. As an example, a friend who suffered from a number of potentially fatal illnesses in the last year of his life, became increasingly tired and unable to concentrate on his work. It is likely that the disease of his blood cells, causing anaemia, was largely responsible. After the surgical accident, described below, the tiredness became more pronounced. Eventually, he slept most of the day, finally lapsing into coma before he died.

With increasing age, the amount we sleep is likely to change. This can go both ways, but usually people who have regularly slept for seven or eight hours a night find they only need five or six hours. They may feel that they 'should' be sleeping for longer because this has always previously been the case. One principle to grasp is that there is no 'should' about length of sleep. The idea of a 'need' for sleep is problematic. Some sleep experts suggest that you are not getting enough sleep if you feel tired during the day. But many older people cope well by sleeping relatively short hours at night and having another 'proper' sleep or a snooze after lunch for an hour or so.

The onset of a terminal illness may affect sleep in a number of different ways. Anxiety about the future may lead to difficulty getting off to sleep, waking in the night or waking early in the morning and lying awake worrying. In contrast, many different types of illness result in increasing tiredness with prolonged sleep at night and a need to sleep during the day. Anaemia or low red blood cells is likely to cause tiredness early on in an illness. Later on, as an illness reaches its terminal phase, usually in the last month or so, most forms of illness are accompanied by increasing tiredness, with eventual slipping into and out of consciousness until finally, often in a coma, the patient dies.

Pain control. For most of our friends, pain was not a prominent feature of their terminal illnesses. When they were afflicted by pain, this was usually relatively easily eased with analgesic medication. This was not the case with one of my friends who suffered a number of fractures of his spine in the last few months of his life. His pain was very difficult to control.

Some terminal conditions do give rise to bad pain. At this stage of life, there is no reason to be stoical about pain. If there are ways of reducing or even removing it, and usually there are, there is no reason to put up with it. You are better off without it. Pain can be acute or chronic. Acute pain occurring, for example, in sharp spasms that only occur intermittently, is more difficult to control than chronic pain. This is because to control severe sharp pain, you need very heavy medication that almost sends you to sleep. You don't want to spend what remains of your life half asleep when most of the time you are not having pain. Some chronic pain, however, is also difficult to relieve. This is particularly the case if it arises because of some neurological problem.

The best person to know how much medication is needed to control your pain is you. Although only a doctor can prescribe medication it is up to you and your family members to make clear that you want really adequate analgesic (pain-relieving) medication to be available at all times. One of my friends suffered from pain at the end of his life quite unnecessarily because a nurse trained to deliver morphine to relieve severe pain could not be found for over twenty-four hours.

One way to ensure timely administration of morphine is available is for the carer to be given a supply and shown how to use it when necessary. This was never provided to any of our friends, except by a German family doctor to our friends in Berlin. The morphine was to be used, the doctor implied, not just for intractable pain but for extreme agitation. In fact, the friend never showed such symptomatology, and his wife never used it.

Swallowing difficulties

In April 2016, I suggested to a friend, a little younger than myself, we should take a short holiday in Dorset. He was becoming increasingly tired and mildly depressed. For over three years he had been suffering from difficulty in swallowing. He had lost a lot of weight. His swallowing difficulty had been extensively investigated without any physical cause being found. I was beginning to think the problem must have a psychological cause. We found an excellent hotel and went for quite long walks over the downs. Dinner in the evening was problematic because of his swallowing problem. I suggested he try one or two techniques derived from cognitive behaviour therapy and they did seem to help a little. I told him that, after our return to London, he really must go and see his GP and, if there was still no physical cause identifiable, he must ask for a referral to a psychiatrist or psychologist. I didn't see him again until early June when he had been to see his GP and been found to be jaundiced, to have very abnormal liver function tests and an enlarged liver. He was found to have a large cancer of the bowel which had spread. He had a colostomy but died only three months later.

Difficulty in swallowing (dysphagia) is a symptom that accompanies many terminal conditions. There may be a feeling of food being stuck in the throat, regurgitation or pain on swallowing. Reduction in the intake of food will lead to loss of weight as it did with my friend. The symptoms may be caused by an obstruction in the mouth, throat (pharynx) or gullet (oesophagus) - the tube leading from the throat to the stomach. The cause may also be neurological. For example, a swallowing problem is quite common after a stroke. Anxiety may also be a cause. Difficulty in swallowing will always need medical assessment with treatment depending on the cause. In many terminal conditions there may be a need for food to be mashed up or served in liquid form or, in more severe cases, for feeding to be through a tube passed down the throat into the stomach.

Incontinence of urine

Cancer of the prostate in one of my friends caused a variety of problems including urine retention, an inability to pass urine. An indwelling catheter was put in place and eventually he had an operation to relieve the blockage. This was ineffective and eventually the catheter was put back.

Inability to control the outflow of urine occurs in the later stages of many terminal illnesses. The cause may be a local problem, for example, an infection or other pathology in the bladder or prostate or be related to excessive production of urine as occurs, for example, in diabetes. It may just be a symptom of extreme tiredness and exhaustion. Some causes, such as urinary infections, are eminently treatable; others are not. If the cause is not treatable, then wearing an incontinence pad may produce a temporary solution. An indwelling catheter as a temporary or permanent measure, may be necessary. In some conditions an opening in the abdomen (a stoma) may be made for the temporary or permanent evacuation of the urine.

Incontinence of faeces

As well as his numerous other symptoms, including great difficulties in communication, swallowing problems and fragility of his bones, my friend with a chronic neurological disease, suffered from incontinence of both urine and faeces. He wore incontinence pads which were relatively effective.

Bowel and bladder incontinence is common in terminal illness. In a study carried out many years ago, Ann Cartwright found that about three in ten people were incontinent of faeces and about the same number incontinent of urine in their last year of life. Though incontinence pads have probably improved over the last fifty years, there is no reason to think much else has changed.as far as these symptoms are concerned.

Because of the smell and messiness, passing motions involuntarily is one of the most embarrassing experiences occurring in terminal illnesses. This was certainly the case with one of my friends and his revulsion for the colostomy was probably one of the reasons why he decided he did not want to pursue the course of chemotherapy that was offered. Like incontinence of urine, faecal incontinence is often a symptom of terminal illness. There may be local causes, such as cancer of the lower part of the intestinal tract, or the symptom may arise as a result of tiredness or exhaustion. If other measures are impracticable, as a temporary or permanent solution, an opening may be made in the abdominal wall. Faeces are then expelled through a small section of the intestinal tract fixed to the outside of the abdomen (ileostomy or colostomy) that leads to a bag which can be regularly emptied.

Other symptoms

There is a great variety of other symptoms occurring in terminal illnesses about which information can be discovered by consulting one of the web sites described above.

3. Avoiding late, pointless interventions

A friend's life was prolonged for several months when he was in serious pain and discomfort by new forms of chemotherapy. Given his poor quality of life, it is very doubtful if these gave him any extension of life which had a reasonable level of quality to it. Of course, these interventions were discussed with him and, given his optimistic personality, he readily agreed, but it is uncertain whether they should have been offered. In contrast, a friend with a rare form of bile duct cancer, was told about the possibility of an extensive operation that would have removed a large amount of her abdominal contents and given a small hope of cure. After a full discussion, she turned it down, a decision which relieved both her family members and quite probably, the surgeons who would have carried out the operation.

The lesson here surely is that when an illness is terminal, it is particularly important that there should be very full discussion between patient, family members and the medical team before any new interventions are embarked upon. Such discussion should take into account levels of unrealistic optimism both in the patient and in their medical advisers.

4. Dealing with medical or surgical mistakes

In two of our friends the cause of death could be put down to a medical or surgical mistake. In one, described above, a significant abnormality on a scan of the abdomen was missed for several months. It is uncertain whether the delay in treatment affected the outcome. Another friend was operated on for the removal of a cancerous nodule in one of his lungs. He had previously had a similar nodule removed successfully. This operation was successful too, but unfortunately, on closing the chest, the surgeon nicked a small artery that runs under the ribs. This in itself might not have caused further damage beyond temporary loss of blood but even more unfortunately, the nursing staff, perhaps because their protocol did not involve sufficiently frequent measurements, did not detect a drop in blood pressure resulting from blood loss in the hours following the operation. By the time the problem was discovered, and the artery repaired, my friend was desperately ill and had to be nursed in intensive care. He never fully recovered and died about two months later, having suffered further bleeding from a duodenal ulcer. Although the cause of his death could not be directly attributed to the surgical accident, it is very likely that it played a major part. His wife and son were naturally angry and indignant about this course of events and lodged a formal complaint. This was clearly the right thing to do. Although mistakes of this sort always lead to internal enquiries, following which there are often policy changes to make sure such mistakes do not recur, receipt of a complaint forces the medical authorities to inform the complainant what went wrong, why it went wrong and what has been done to make sure there is no recurrence.

Personal and family issues

1. How to deal with feelings of dependency

Among our friends, it was the loss of independence that struck hardest in their final illnesses. When she described the most difficult part of looking after her husband, one wife recounted how difficult she found it to watch him do up his shirt buttons. Though weak and frail, he was determined to do this on his own, no matter how long it took him. She got so impatient with him, she could hardly restrain herself from saying 'Oh, come on, let me do it.' In these circumstances, knowing how much he would hate this, she would find some excuse to leave the room for a few minutes until she had regained her equilibrium. Another widow described how, even though he had pain in his back following a fracture, for her husband the worst part of his terminal illness was the humiliation that accompanied his incontinence and the fact that he needed help to keep himself clean. In the initial stages of his illness, my friend with a chronic neurological disorder insisted on going to the doctor by himself. This meant that his wife never quite knew whether the account he gave of the likely progression of his condition was accurate or over-influenced by her husband's optimistic personality. As another friend's sight and hearing deteriorated from her seventies onwards, her children always wanted to go along to appointments with opticians and audiologists so that they could help their mother work out how best to deal with her cataracts and hearing problems. Without their input they suspect she remained cut off from the outside world far more than she need have been. It was only when she was admitted to a residential home for a short period towards the very end of her life that her vision and hearing were properly assessed and treated with very positive results.

Increasing dependency is an almost inevitable part of the dying process. It happens because, during most terminal illnesses, the person becomes increasingly weaker, losing muscle power because the muscles are gradually wasting away. Eventually it becomes impossible for the person to feed or dress themselves or attend to their own toilet needs. Perhaps surprisingly, this is often the hardest part of dying. In the UK at the time of writing, it is not legal to have assistance from a health professional to end one's life if one has had enough of it. But increasingly, throughout the world, assisted dying has been legalised and there is a great deal we can learn from those countries where this is the case (see Chapter 8). In 1994, with its Death with Dignity Act, Oregon was the first American state to legalise this practice. When the Oregon authorities review the reasons why people with terminal illness opt for a health professional assisted death, the main reason given by over 90% of those who request it is not agonising pain or fear of suffocation or any other set of physical symptoms, but 'loss of autonomy'.

The importance we give to our independence is, in fact, not surprising at all. From our earliest days, at least in western societies, we are given praise for doing things without help. Throughout the whole of the life span, there is a premium given to people able to do things on their own. When toddlers take their first steps on their own, they are usually inundated with praise. When the lives of centenarians are described, it is their capacity to do their own shopping, to sort out their own household bills, to write their own emails, that are regarded as the most remarkable features of their lives.

This emphasis on the desirability of being self-sufficient, independent, is not universal. It is particular to western societies. In other cultures, where it is the social group rather than the individual that is given greater value, to be dependent on other people and to have other people dependent on oneself is regarded as a normal, indeed a desirable part of life. Being dutiful, loyal, and sharing are values thought to be more important than individual achievement and self-sufficiency.

What are the best ways of maintaining the self-respect of dying people in the face of increasing frailty? First, they need to be involved in making decisions that are going to affect their own lives for as long as possible. Even if they can only answer 'yes' or 'no' by nodding or shaking their heads, they can still participate in deciding when to eat or drink. If they cannot fully manage their own toilet needs, they can be shown appreciation for cooperating in helping while these are being attended to. This is often difficult. For example, my friend with a chronic neurological disorder lost his voice many months before he died. He was so weak that even getting him to spell out his wishes was a challenge, but great efforts were made by all his carers to help him to do so. As we have seen, the cancer of the tongue suffered by another friend meant that his voice eventually reduced in volume to a barely audible whisper but again, everyone involved in his care tried to ensure they knew what he wanted. Our friends were always given a voice when it came to decisions about future medical interventions and care and were generally, though not always quick to refuse any treatment when the benefits were uncertain, and the risk of distressing side effects was high. When a friend was told she should stay in hospital for investigations a month or so before her death, her preference for returning home was honoured without question. In general, hospital doctors treated patients in this way, but this was not always helpful. A consultant who had never met him before asked a confused friend of mine very near the end of his life if he would like to be resuscitated even if it was likely that successful resuscitation resulted in his surviving as a 'vegetable'. Even though, when fully compos mentis, this friend had said that he wouldn't, on this occasion, because of his confusion, he said that he would. It required an intervention by his son to sort the matter out so that he retained his 'Do not resuscitate' notice at the end of the bed.

In some circumstances, it is difficult to avoid a sense of humiliation in terminally ill patients. This is particularly the case when there is double incontinence. However, some carers successfully managed to do this by carrying out the 'clearing up' operations gently and with minimal fuss and responding to the patients' apologies for the trouble they were causing by saying it was a privilege and gave real satisfaction to be able to help in this way. Except by being as cooperative as possible, patients cannot share in many of the physical aspects of their care but there is much greater opportunity for reciprocity in the emotional nature of the relationships between carers and patients. For example, patients can and our friends often did share with their partners nearly until their end in the pleasures and disappointments in the lives of their children and grandchildren as well as the family members of their professional carers.

My friend with a chronic neurological disorder who was highly dependent on others for his care attended weekly art therapy classes at his local hospice for four years. Some of the titles he gave his works provides an insight into how he felt about himself: 'De Profundis', 'A glimpse of paradise' which included a ladder, and 'I nearly forgot my ladder' for one that didn't. His creations were lively and often symbolic. He was delighted when some were exhibited at the Royal Academy, but what was perhaps more important was that art therapy enabled him to communicate with a skilled therapist. Of course, art therapy will not be available for more than a small minority of people with terminal illness, but a whole variety of activities as well as painting and drawing, such as listening to music, watching old films on the small screen and then talking about them, can heighten self-esteem as well as give much pleasure.

If dying people had responsibilities before they became terminally ill, they should be encouraged to retain these roles for just as long as they are competent to do so. 'Going gentle' does not mean giving up on activities that are rewarding and enjoyable as soon as a terminal illness is diagnosed. Far from it. One friend remained Chair of a school governing body and of the Public Monuments Association until very near the end. Another only resigned as Chair of the governing body of a local primary school during her very last hospital admission. Another remained a member of the

Spoliation Advisory Panel, a body set up to advise on the disposal of works of art looted by the Nazis until she was ninety years old and her hearing impairment made meetings difficult for her.

There are also ways in which, long before they face their terminal illnesses, people need to prepare for the time when they or their partners may be in this position. One of the striking features of the marriages of our friends, which is much less true for the next generation is the very striking division of labour according to gender. Though a small number of the wives contributed significantly to the family income, largely speaking it was the men who earned the household income, paid the bills and looked after the structure and maintenance of the family house. The women did most of the childcare, the shopping and cooking and either did the household tasks themselves or organised cleaning help. When the last illness supervened, if it was the man who was affected, unless he had developed dementia, he was able to carry on paying the bills etc until near the end. Generally, the wives did not need to take over until death. In some cases however, they did take over managing the family finances. When this happened, they were usually able to do this without great difficulty. One husband, noting this and appreciating his wife's competence for the first time and, it has to be said, just in time, said to her – 'I think I've underestimated you.' In the smaller number of cases in which it was the wife who was dying, mostly in the last few weeks or months it was possible to bring in other members of the family or paid help to perform the household tasks and cooking. Where this presented a problem, husbands showed a striking incapacity to take over. With one exception, to be described below, none of the husbands had done more in the way of cooking than boiling an egg or making a cup of tea. Mostly this did not matter; other hands were willing to help, but in one case a terminally ill wife could not accept the complete ineptitude of her husband when it came to preparing a meal under her instruction. This led to the first episodes of serious tension and disharmony in what had been a long and strikingly affectionate marriage. The problem was that what had been a perfectly satisfactory balance of responsibilities had been upset with unfortunate consequences. If the husband had learned how to cook, his wife could have been spared the extreme irritability she experienced when she became too incapacitated to cook and he was unable to take over. When one partner becomes frail, as at some time will inevitably be the case, there are major advantages if the other can take over. My own wife made a well-timed intervention in this direction when she enrolled me on a cookery course as a present on my sixtieth birthday. Since then, I have done my fair share of the cooking.

More generally, there needs to be a change in the value given to cooperation and sharing over competitive success and this needs to take place early in life. Coping with dependency would be a whole lot easier if, before our terminal illnesses, we lived lives in which it was accepted we care for each other and that being cared for is just as much a legitimate source of pleasure as caring for others. In some primary school classrooms, the achievements of the individual child are subordinated to the good of the group. Praise is given to the whole class if everyone achieves a good level of attainment rather than to the individuals who are outstanding. This means that all children try to help those who find the work most difficult. It's a good start. After school, there is now increasing emphasis on cooperation in the workplace as the key to business success. The need to make teamwork part of the workplace culture, to provide teams with the resources they need to work together, to ensure joint learning in training programmes and to encourage socialising outside of work hours are all seen as ways of increasing cooperation and thus business success. In this way, helping others and being helped by them can became more valued than being successful.

2. Providing emotional support

Terminal illness is the occasion for the greatest loss we ever experience, the loss of our lives. As the end approaches, we may well be relieved that we shall suffer pain and discomfort no longer, but such relief can never remove though it may soften our sense of loss. Knowing that one will no longer be able to share the pleasures and problems of life with one's partner if one has one, with one's children, if one has them, but, in any case with other relatives and friends is inevitably an incredibly tough call. There may well be particular events in the future one will be sad to miss, the birth of a grandchild or great grandchild, the sharing of next

Christmas, maybe just lunches with an old friend, reliving memories. Whatever we shall be missing, we need emotional support and understanding at this time of our lives. So, of course, will those closest to us need such support in their loss of us.

Perhaps the most important part of what my late friends brought to their final illness, was their close family and friendships. Of our twenty-four friends who have died during recent years, twenty-two, the great majority, had been married and living continuously with their spouses, (in all but one case their first spouse), for at least forty years. Three women had been widowed, one fairly recently and the other two for over forty-five years, and one woman had never married. Although the rate of divorce was much lower in this generation than in the one that followed it, even so, this represents a very high level of marital stability. My interview did not involve any probing into the quality of the marriages of my friends. This would have been inappropriate. All the same, it was clear from the interviews and indeed from what I already knew, that, generally speaking, the husbands and wives of our friends provided an enormously high level of both emotional and physical support during this last illness. Many, perhaps most of the spouses to all intents and purposes gave up their lives to provide company, keep the home going and generally look after their dying partner. Similarly, though clearly at a lower level of intensity, adult children and friends almost universally provided a significant amount of emotional support. Many children rang each day for an update of how the illness was progressing and often gave helpful advice when problems arose. They came whenever they could.

The way emotional support was provided is difficult to describe. My relatively brief interview was not designed to elicit such information, but inevitably much was spontaneously forthcoming. Most of my interviewees were the surviving spouses themselves and it was not to be expected that they would describe just how much sympathetic care they themselves had provided. But it was clear from what they said that they had all done their utmost to make sure that their dying partner knew he or she was deeply loved. Spouses willingly endured countless sleepless nights and shared the deep disappointments of failed treatments before the end came. For a small number of spouses, the strain was just too much, and they had to go away for periods of time to regain their energies before they could resume their caring roles. All spouses were able to share the emotional stress with other members of the family and friends. For nearly all, communication by email, text and WhatsApp was a daily occurrence over the last few weeks. Naturally, not all family members and friends agreed with the course of treatment that was being followed. Some were full of advice that had, almost always, already been considered. Explaining why certain lines of intervention had not been followed sometimes laid a further burden on the main carer. This may make it sound as if family members and friends were largely unhelpful and this was not the case. But there were indeed times when help offered with the best of intentions was unwelcome. It was clear from the interviews that dying is not just the experience of an individual, but a social experience, and that the complications of the relationships with family members and friends are often an integral part of the terminal period.

One of the surprising features of the terminal illnesses of our friends is that none received any professional help from counsellors or mental health professionals to deal with feelings of anxiety or depression.

3. Recognising the importance of what people bring to their terminal illness.

One possible reason why my Parisian friend was resilient in the face of his death was that he had survived a serious threat to his life much earlier on. As a Jewish child in France, he had gone into hiding with his parents to escape capture and probably extermination by Nazi Germans during the Second World War. For ever after that, he felt the remainder of his life was a bonus. Another friend had had a similar experience as a Jewish child whose family had protected him against capture by the Nazis. He had emigrated from Vienna to Holland and then to London, having to learn three different languages in a year and undergoing several separations from his father. This particular friend's experience as a farmer was also relevant. He had had to 'put down' several animals who were suffering distress as a result of illness during his career. He had never had any doubt that this was the right thing to do and compared this behaviour with his feelings about his own need to die when his time had come. Another friend had suffered a melanoma, a cancer particularly likely to recur after a long period of remission, in his thirties. Both he and his wife felt lucky that he had survived for so long after this first cancer diagnosis. Another friend had survived a diagnosis of Guillain-Barré Syndrome, a condition producing gradual paralysis of all the muscles in the body, which very nearly killed him in his fifties. At the age of seven, another friend had been one of the last children to be evacuated from Germany on a kinder transport in 1939. Both his parents were killed in a concentration camp while he himself was adopted by a British family. All these friends were 'steeled' and made more resilient by their earlier life-threatening experiences.

But perhaps the most influential part of ourselves that enable us to 'go gentle' in our terminal illnesses are our personalities. Among the more relevant personality features is the degree of acceptance of one's fate, whatever that might be. Some of my friends fought vigorously against their illness until almost the very end believing they could beat off their cancerous enemy. Others, with the same diagnosis, such as he who said 'If the good Lord wants to take me over the waterfall of life, so be it', were more accepting of their fate. Some of our friends were incredibly stoical despite suffering dreadfully distressing symptomatology unrelieved by excellent medical and nursing care. Others, especially those with anxious, hypochondriacal personalities were much less tolerant of what seemed more minor inconvenience. Willingness to spend money or determination to lay out as little as possible were also important personality features. All our friends had enough money to ensure good medical treatment and care for themselves, but some were, not to put too fine a point on it, meaner than others and suffered as a result because of inadequate care. In general, personality features were sharpened rather than softened by the experience of serious illness.

One friend was always particularly independent-minded. As a member of the Communist Party in the 1940s and early 1950s, she had stood outside mainstream politics. As a developmental psychologist, she had had to withstand deep hostility because of her support for adoptions of young children of colour into white British families when no adoptive parents of colour were available. When she became frail, I well remember how firmly she rejected my offer to hold her arm in support when we crossed the road near her flat. Then, in the last few weeks of her life, she turned down the offer of a hospital bed, preferring to go back to her own flat where she lived alone rather than risk being, as she saw it, institutionalised in a hospital. She always said she did not mind the idea of dying alone and indeed this is what happened.

Another friend had always been a sweet-tempered woman whose first thoughts were for others. As well as her professional work in fostering and adoption, she was involved in all sorts of voluntary work for her church and in the local community. She did not give up being Chair of Governors of her local primary school until the late stages of her terminal illness. In her last weeks, she was uncomplaining, only experiencing delight and pleasure in being able to have her children close to her in the hospice where she spent her last days.

A significant amount of the distress occurring in the terminal illnesses of our friends arose because of their personalities, sometimes stubbornly independent to a fault so that they would not accept help that would have been readily forthcoming, sometimes quite unable to accept the fact that they were indeed going to die and so unwilling to take the necessary steps to ensure a fitting end. If you resolutely refuse to accept you are going on a one-way journey, you can't say goodbye. Some of my friends brought a particular expectation of length of life to their last days. Jonathan Miller when interviewed in his sixties, said he thought if he lived until he was eighty, he would have had as long a life as he might reasonably expect. In fact, nearly all our friends survived until their eighties and, if asked, would say they had had what is popularly called 'a good innings'.

The fact that our dying friends experienced their terminal illnesses in their eighties and that their spouses were of a similar age made it inevitable that many of their partners had health problems of their own which made caring even more difficult than it otherwise might have been. The two problems that interfered most with the care given by spouses were joint and memory problems. One friend's final illness only lasted about three or four months. For some months before this, because of his wife's hip problems, he had had to do some of the cooking and take some of the responsibility for keeping the house clean. Once he himself became seriously ill, the children had to make other arrangements for cooking and cleaning. Once another friend developed dementia, she could no longer cope with the cooking and cleaning. Her husband might have been able to help to some degree, but he himself developed a rapidly progressive dementia, so that the only solution was to bring in full-time, twenty-four hour a day care. Eventually even this arrangement became untenable, and the wife went into residential care before she died. After some months, the husband himself also needed to go into residential care where, at the time of writing, seven years after his wife's death, he remains

4. Divorce, separation, social isolation, loneliness

Only one of our friends who had recently died had been divorced or separated. This particular friend had been married for twenty-five years before he and his first wife separated and shortly afterwards, divorced. They had two daughters, in their fifties at the time of his terminal illness. After the divorce, they had remained in closer contact with their mother than with their father. He remarried shortly after the divorce was finalised. He and his second wife continued to live in Israel for over twenty years before emigrating to Berlin because of increasing dislike of Israeli government policies.

After they had been living in Germany for about three years, he developed a vascular form of dementia (see Chapter 7). Although there was some minor loss of memory, his incapacities mainly took the form of difficulties managing the couple's financial affairs and loss of ability to find his way around. On a small number of occasions, he wandered out of the flat and had to be brought home. Once he was lost for over twenty-four hours and was located by the police in a dishevelled state in a hostel for the homeless. In the last six or seven months of his life, he developed a lung condition and had to receive 24-hour oxygen before eventually, he died.

After their separation and divorce, he and his first wife had communicated very little with each other and his relationship with his daughters was not at all close, though he was delighted to hear from them and talk with them. Communication though was mainly confined to occasional letters and emails. After he developed dementia, his second wife kept his daughters informed of the progress of his condition. Both daughters came to see him in Berlin occasionally and one of them visited him for three weeks during the later stages of his illness and was most helpful to his second wife, but otherwise there was very little contact between him and his daughters. They did not attend the ceremony arranged to inter his ashes in a wood even though a considerable attempt was made to arrange this at a time convenient for them. My friend himself did not seem particularly upset by the very limited contact between him, his daughters and his grandchildren.

The extremely low rate of divorce and separation among our late friends requires some explanation. At the present time, about half contracted marriages end in divorce. Much of the increase in the rate of divorce in the UK followed the passing of the 1969 Divorce Reform Act which came into effect in 1971. This made it much easier for couples to obtain a divorce. However, the main reason why our late friends divorced so infrequently was that they came from stable backgrounds themselves and were good at making long-lasting relationships. Further, Jews have a lower divorce rate than other groups and a significant proportion of our friends were Jewish or part-Jewish.

In future generations a much larger number of people with terminal illnesses will have been separated or divorced in the past. They will have children from previous relationships. Most will have entered into second or third marriages and will have partners, but some will be living alone. This will result, indeed is already resulting in some highly problematic situations. If a terminally ill man has not had contact with a former wife for some years, should she be informed when he becomes terminally ill? If they had children together, from whom he has been estranged or with whom he has had little contact, should they be told how ill he is? Then there is the question of visiting the terminally ill person. The fact that someone only has a short time to live means that this is the last chance for explanations and forgiveness. Then, after the death, there is the often-difficult question of attendance at the funeral. Who is to be invited?

How these difficult situations are managed will depend on an almost infinite variety of possible situations. At one extreme, the terminally ill person may be completely estranged from his or her former family and may not even know how to contact them. At the other extreme, there may still be very friendly relationships between the former and the present relationship with frequent visiting and affectionate contact. The first partner may have formed other partnerships or be living alone. There may or may not be children and grandchildren of the former relationship. In cases where the terminally ill person has contracted three or four marriages or been in this number of stable cohabitations, the situation is, of course, even more complicated. On the one hand, terminal illness offers a final opportunity for repair of damaged relationships. On the other, unfortunately, terminal illness is also not infrequently the occasion for the development of even greater embitterment than had existed beforehand.

A French friend in her late sixties was involved in the complexities of a terminal illness when the dying person had had multiple long-lasting partnerships. She had lived with a partner for fifteen years while they were in their thirties and forties. Their partnership ended painfully but they had remained in touch mainly by telephone, email and occasional meetings ever since. She had had a son by a previous marriage and had a further son by her now dying partner. Shortly after the breakup with this partner, she had developed a long-lasting relationship with and married another man, who himself had three children by two previous marriages. After the relationship between her and the now terminally ill partner broke down, he had met and married another woman. He had himself been previously married to another woman, who, after their breakup, herself formed a relationship with another man who had six children.

Three years before he died in 2018, her former partner had developed a cough which turned out to be a symptom of lung cancer. During his terminal illness, my friend and her husband provided much emotional support. This was necessary as the terminally ill man's wife had serious personality problems and was unable to provide such support herself. The situation was complicated by the fact that the son of the dying man felt angry with my friend's son by a previous marriage, for taking too little interest in his step-father's serious illness. After death, the arrangements for the funeral were made by one of the children the deceased man had had with his first wife. My friend had never met this first wife before, but when they did meet, the two became good friends and have remained in touch ever since. Such complex patterns of relationships of such variable quality are unusual today but are likely to become much more frequent in the future.

The possibility that either the terminally ill person or a former partner is living alone brings with it a likelihood of social isolation, always a significant additional stress when a life is coming to an end. As the situation of my late friends well illustrates, however, the lack of a live-in partner by no means implies that someone living alone will be socially isolated and lonely. Before he died in 1995, Geoffrey Warnock told his wife he felt almost a duty to depart this world because his wife was so perfectly cut out for the life of a widow. Indeed, after his death, Mary Warnock lived a highly productive, enjoyable and sociable life until her death twenty-four years later. Another friend, on the death of her husband in 1979, embarked on the most productive part of her professional career and enjoyed a very full life until her own death thirty-six years later. Of course, the death of a spouse may be followed by deep and unhappy loneliness for many years either as a result of a long-lasting bereavement reaction or for other reasons. A son described to me how his father had been what he called the 'passport' to his mother's social life during their long marriage. When the husband died in 2003, his widow found it difficult to socialise and suffered from loneliness until her own death in 2021 eighteen years later. Those who have lived alone for years may suffer their terminal illnesses in a state of deep deprivation of social contact. The son of one of my late friends is chief executive of Pathway, a charity that aims to meet the health needs of the homeless. Relatively recently, this charity has sought to embed palliative care services into hostels for the homeless in an attempt to meet the needs of the dying who are homeless.

5. Tailoring expectations to the realities of the future

One of the issues which my interviews illuminated was the place of diagnosis in the trajectory of a terminal illness. We tend to think in terms of a medical journey ending in death which begins with the appearance of some worrying symptoms. The person showing the symptoms then identifies himself or herself as a patient and goes to the doctor for advice. The doctor examines the patient, carries out some investigations and may refer for specialist hospital advice. At the end of this investigatory phase, a diagnosis is made and, if there are treatments available for the condition diagnosed, these are begun. If these are unsuccessful, the patient dies. For a whole variety of reasons, this classical medical journey just did not occur with most of our friends. This was rarely because of medical incompetence, but much more frequently either because a diagnosis was difficult to make or because symptoms that turned out to indicate fatal disease affected someone who was already showing signs of chronic ill-health.

So, for example, the friend I have already described who suffered from difficulties in swallowing for at least three years before he died had them thoroughly investigated but no physical problem was identified to account for them. Eventually, only four months before he died, he went to his family doctor with the same symptoms which, by now had resulted in serious loss of weight. He was found to be jaundiced and clearly seriously ill. The problem was rapidly identified as a cancer of the bowel, which proved fatal despite an operation for its removal. The cause of the swallowing problems which must have had some relevance remained mysterious until the end. Another friend had a long period lasting many years of poor health with diabetes and back problems. Her back was extremely painful, but she experienced significant relief with steroid injections and on one occasion from an operation. Then, only a few weeks before she died, a scan of her abdomen unexpectedly revealed a large lump in her liver. This turned out to be a cancer, not, as is usually the case with lumps in the liver, a secondary growth from elsewhere, but a primary liver cancer. Only a fortnight later, when I visited, she was obviously dreadfully ill and wanted to give me instructions as to what to include when I wrote her obituary. Less than a fortnight further on, she died in the local hospice. In neither of these two cases could it be said that there was the slightest hint of medical incompetence, yet in both cases the condition which caused death had clearly been present, undiagnosed, for at least several weeks and probably months before death. This was the rule rather than the exception among my friends.

The speed of the medical journey to its final end varied greatly even with similar or identical diagnoses. For example, one couple both suffered from dementia. The husband's loss of memory began in his mid-seventies and has very gradually deteriorated since that time. Now, at the time of writing, about fifteen years after the onset of his dementia, he is in residential care. In contrast, his wife only began to develop loss of memory when she was about eighty, but her cognitive abilities declined very rapidly. She also had heart disease and suffered a number of mini-strokes. Within two years she had died.

6. Recognising the finality of the terminal illness

With nearly all our friends, the fact that the end of their lives was approaching was understood at different points in time by them, by their close relatives and by friends. In all cases, except that of the one friend who died suddenly and unexpectedly, there was inevitably in the months preceding death, a good deal of uncertainty as to when precisely the end would come. Such uncertainty was usually removed only a few days or a week or two before death when it became clear there was only a very short time to go. In the usually months-long period of awareness that this illness would prove terminal, but uncertainty remained about when death would occur, there was usually an implicit acceptance that time left was limited. Usually at the insistence of the terminally ill person, plans would be made for what would happen after death. This was the time when, if at all, know-how about financial management, wishes about the details of the funeral were expressed and even thoughts about who might speak at a memorial celebration were shared (see Chapter 9). This was a time for hand-holding but not, among my friends at least, usually the expression of affection or other emotions. For example, as I have already described, one friend, long widowed, talked to her children about her lack of concern that she might die alone with no one with her. This is indeed what happened for she died in her sleep and the first anyone knew about her death was when she was found lifeless one morning.

There was a small number of our friends who never reached a point of openly sharing awareness, either implicitly or explicitly that death was close. If, during the interview, I broached the subject of communicating with the dying friend about the approach of death, the relative would, in these cases, express horror at the thought. There were feelings both that this would be cruel, and that the dying person would not wish to know. This attitude meant that there were no opportunities for planning for after the death. When, in the interview, I suggested this must have had disadvantages, it was clear that these were seen as small and insignificant in comparison to the emotional difficulties of more open communication.

Couples who did not share an acceptance that death was near must surely be seen as, at least to some degree, to have been 'in denial'. There is sometimes an assumption that denial is an inappropriate reaction to bad news, at least partly because it is thought that people in denial are likely to suffer severe depression, anxiety and other emotional reactions that they would be spared if only they were able to face reality. My observations on this very limited sample suggest that those couples who were apparently 'in denial' or did not want to talk about their own impending deaths did not seem to show different emotional reactions from others who were more open in dealing with the sad facts of death. On the other hand, the surviving relatives of 'deniers' were undoubtedly more often left with more 'loose ends' or uncertainty about what the terminally ill person would have wanted in a number of different circumstances.

Another problem arose because the recognition of the finality of an illness often varied greatly between our now deceased friend, their close family members and the doctor or doctors. Typically, after the presentation of symptoms, doctors would have a reasonable, but by no means precise idea just how soon the condition would prove fatal, if indeed it proved fatal at all. In most cases they did not communicate information about the possibility of fatality at this early stage to the patient or to the rest of the family in very clear terms, partly because of reticence, partly out of denial and significantly because they did not have a very clear idea themselves. As symptoms worsened, so typically family members would press for a clearer idea of the future. Then eventually, (and sometimes this never occurred before death), our friends themselves would learn their fate.

Dealing with the very end of life

The last weeks and days of a person's life have particular significance not only for the person who is dying but for those who remain. They are always memorable and may be charged with regrets and guilt, with a satisfying sense of a fitting end or with something in between.

In her well-received book on dying and death, the highly experienced palliative care physician, Kathryn Mannix, describes a conversation the leader of a hospice team had with a French woman with a terminal illness who was highly anxious about the suffering she thought she would experience in her last days and hours. 'As time goes by,' he explains, 'people become more tired, more weary ... What we expect to happen from now on is that you will just be progressively more tired and you will need longer sleeps, and spend less time awake. As time goes by,' he goes on, 'we find that people begin to spend more time sleeping, and some of that time they are even more deeply asleep, they slip into a coma. I mean they are unconscious ... And so, at the very end of life, a person is simply unconscious all of the time ... And then their breathing starts to change ... No sudden rush of pain at the end. No feeling of fading away. No panic. Just very, very peaceful.' Naturally, the patient is greatly reassured (pp 23-24).

This description of a tranquil end matches well the experience of most of our friends, but not with a significant minority. One, the earlier phase of whose terminal illness has already been described, suffered from cancer of the tongue which prevented him from speaking and swallowing. He had to be tube fed. He suffered extreme discomfort in his mouth and face, only partially relieved by medication. Five days before he died, he moved into a local hospice where he was put on increasing amounts of pain-relieving medication. His family members were allowed to visit as often as they wanted. As described earlier in this chapter, he was one of the very few practising Christians among my friends and was calmed by a visit from a Methodist minister. After slipping into a coma his breathing gradually became less regular and, surrounded by his family, it finally stopped. His end came without any apparent distress.

Six years later, his widow moved into the local hospice where her husband had previously been nursed and died. According to her children, the care was 'fantastic'. One or other member of the family was with her for 18-20 hours a day. She also was visited by a Methodist minister in the days before she died. With the progress of her illness and increasing medication, gradually she slept for longer and longer periods and slipped into unconsciousness. Her breaths became less frequent and eventually stopped completely. Her children felt this was exactly the sort of death she would have wanted for herself.

A number of our friends had a similar end of life, free from distress or pain. This was certainly the case for the friend who died virtually instantaneously. He was found to have died in his study less than half an hour after finishing a game of online bridge. Another friend was found to have died probably in her sleep, when one of her daughters visited her the morning after she had spent an evening with her. A number of other friends died at home after gradually losing consciousness, usually with one or more family members present at the end. In some cases, the family member I interviewed was unable to give me an account of the last few hours of our friend's life as death had occurred in hospital some time after the last visit. There is every reason to think, however, that these deaths followed the same pattern.

In at least three of our friends however, the end did not come in this tranquil manner. A few weeks before he died, one friend had an operation to remove a cancer of the bowel He was left with a colostomy which he hated. Although he was able to manage it himself, he hated it, finding dealing with it a disgusting business. He made it clear that if he collapsed, he did not want to be resuscitated. 'If this is living,' he said, 'I do not want any more of it.'. When he was in severe discomfort some days before he died, for a day or two it proved impossible to find a nurse who was qualified to deliver morphine. Finally, one was found and he had intravenous morphine for the last twenty four hours of his life.

How do hospice, hospital and home care compare in terms of quality of care at the very end of life?

Those of our friends who spent the last few days or weeks before they died in a hospice all had a good and, in most cases, an excellent experience. Almost inevitably this was a period when, to ease agitation or physical symptoms, adequate sedation had to be administered. This was more or less guaranteed in a hospice where the dying person was usually given control with a self-administered morphine drip or, if this was not possible, qualified nursing was always available to ensure it was given adequately. The hospices had a policy of allowing, indeed encouraging 24/7 visiting, so that the dying person needed only be alone for short periods. A small number of our friends had such complicated nursing needs in the last few days of life that care in a hospice or hospital was really necessary.

The availability of hospice care was fortunate for them because, as far as end-of-life care was concerned, the experience of our friends who finished their lives in hospital was much more variable. Their experiences were sometimes good, usually because the dying person slipped in and out of coma and needed little nursing care. But one or two had an apparently agonising last few days with inadequate nursing and a hit and miss visiting policy. About half our friends died at home either because hospice care was not available or because there was a strong wish to end life in familiar surroundings. Again, experience was very variable. Because visiting was not a problem, it largely depended on the quality of palliative care or community nursing. These professionals were often too stretched to provide a good service and there were also problems arising from lack of continuity of care. Some of these problems were probably unavoidable, but, as far as possible, relatives of people who are dying and wish to spend their last weeks and days at home should, as far as possible, plan ahead to ensure that sedation is, to the maximum degree possible, self-administered and that there is consistent nursing care with continuity of the professional staff involved. This is not always possible. The last weeks of one of our friends were spent in Berlin but the care he received was typical of much delivered in the UK. His wife reported that while the medical and nursing care he received was excellent, this was far from the case as far as his social care was concerned.

One can conclude that, if the criterion of a good quality at the end of life is effective symptom control, then this is achieved in most cases, but not in a significant minority. If the criterion is good quality of care, then this too is usually achieved, but deficiencies in the care system mean this is far from a universal experience.

CHAPTER 7

Improving the quality of life of the terminally ill person with dementia

Introduction

A quarter, or six out of the twenty-four of our close friends who have died recently had advanced dementia in their last months of life. This is about the expected rate for people in their eighties. It is surprising however that the rate was as high as it was as an advanced level of education is meant to be protective against dementia and nearly all my friends were university-educated. In contrast to all the other illnesses that have ended my friends' lives, dementia has posed especially difficult problems both to the terminally ill person and to those family members caring for them. In some ways, the presence of dementia makes 'going gentle' easier, in others, more difficult.

Normal brain ageing

Dementia must be distinguished from the deterioration of memory that occurs in nearly all of us as we reach our sixties and seventies. We begin to lose neurones in our teens and twenties when brain-shaping takes place. This loss continues throughout life though memory decline is not usually detectable until much later in life. Nearly all my friends noticed some degree of deterioration in their memories before they reached their eighties. In an essay she wrote called 'On Being 88' a few months before she died, my late friend Barbara Tizard wrote:

> I have also read poetry since I was about ten, when I discovered the delights of long narrative poems such as The Highwayman, and The Lady of Shallot. At that age I could effortlessly (or so I remember it) commit long passages to memory. At school in my teens, when daily ball games were compulsory, I would ostentatiously walk around the pitch reciting poetry – this cannot have endeared me to my classmates, but they accepted me as an eccentric. Now, I usually read one or two poems in bed before putting my light out. I have tried memorising them as I did as a child, but I forget them so quickly that I have abandoned the attempt.

As we move into our sixties and seventies, we most of us sense we are not as sharp as we were. If we are driving, we may note we have to concentrate on the road more and not be distracted by what is happening on either side of the road. We may forget what day of the week it is and have to remind ourselves. We are more likely to go upstairs or into another room and then have forgotten why we made the journey. We may find more difficulty remembering the names of people with whom we are really very familiar. Before immediately realising our mistake, we may put biscuits in the fridge and milk in the cupboard rather than the other way round. Things seem to get lost more easily; we forget where we have put our spectacles or the TV remote controls. Often these apparent lapses of memory are really more to do with lack of attention. We are thinking of something else when we put our glasses down and so when we want to pick them up again, we haven't registered where we have put them as our minds were elsewhere.

We may occasionally forget an arrangement we have made. It is important to bear in mind that, unless we have been very exceptional people in our younger days, all these minor problems have arisen before throughout our lives. What are frequently called 'senior moments' are probably not all that new. If we are honest, most of us will remember 'junior moments' in our twenties when we have struggled to remember a name or where we have put a book we have mislaid. I still cringe at the memory of an intensely embarrassing experience when I was in my early fifties. One January lunchtime my secretary (this was in the days when hospital consultants had secretaries) rang through to my office to ask where I was. I told her she knew perfectly well where I was. I was in my office next door to hers in London. 'Well,' she said, 'you ought to be in Macclesfield giving a lecture. They've just phoned through to ask where you were.' I had failed to transfer the arrangement into my new diary. How much these 'senior moments' trouble us is more a matter of personality than of objective memory loss. Studies of people in their seventies suggest that worry about memory loss is more related to having an anxious personality than to poor performance in memory testing.

Prevention

An increased tendency to forget things needs to be countered by some, perhaps rather minor changes in our habits. When going shopping for say half a dozen items in one's twenties one may well be able to carry a list of what one needs in one's head. By one's sixties it is as well to make a written list. It becomes a good idea to check one's diary each morning for arrangements one has made for that day. Though the evidence for its effectiveness is not very strong, it's probably a good idea to involve oneself at least once or twice a week in mind-stretching exercises such a playing a game of computer chess or tackling Sudoku at an appropriate level of difficulty. Forgetting the names of the children of one's friends is a common problem, so write down their names beside that of the relevant phone numbers in your address book. Reading keeps the brain active but passive reading will not do much for your brain. Making a short daily diary entry, perhaps including a few lines about what you have been reading, is likely to be more effective.

Apart from keeping the brain active, there are other ways in which one can reduce the risk of developing dementia. One helpful aphorism goes 'what is good for the heart is good for the brain.' This is not surprising as an important influence on the dementing process is the state of the arteries supplying the brain. So, taking regular exercise, maintaining a weight that is healthy for one's age and height and not smoking all reduce the risk of dementia. It is probably safest not to drink alcohol at all over the age of 70 as even small amounts of alcohol act as a weak neurotoxin. More unexpectedly, having regular checks on one's hearing and actually wearing hearing aids rather than just being in possession of them, makes dementia less likely. This is probably because unless one can hear well, one is less likely to have conversations with other people and these play an important part in stimulating the brain.

As I've noted earlier in this chapter, Barbara Tizard wrote in her essay 'On Being 88' that she could no longer memorise poetry as she had done in her childhood. But in fact, that by no means describes the full extent of her cognitive decline. In her last few months, she rather frequently muddled up the names of her two daughters and her granddaughter. She could not manage to cook as well as she had done in the past (she had been a very good cook) and indeed lost interest in food. She couldn't manage a new cooker which had been bought for her as her old one was no longer working properly. She sometimes couldn't really understand what people said to her. She may well have been showing early signs of dementia, but she continued to read and attend her book club to which she contributed relevantly. She managed to cope with visitors who came to stay in her flat.

This friend probably managed to continue to function as well as she did because she used many of the coping strategies I have mentioned above. She started to do crosswords, an activity she had derided in the past and kept a book on her kitchen table in which she wrote down appointments and lists of things she needed to buy. She got her daughters to check she had paid her bills. She went out every day to a local café and talked to people she recognised when they passed by. She discovered that if she did not understand what people said to her, for example nurses in a hospital department, if she just smiled at them, they just seemed to accept her response and go away.

Signs and course of dementia

More serious problems with memory and behaviour are likely to be a sign of dementia. In the early stages of dementia, a person may become much more forgetful, especially of things that have just happened. They may ask when breakfast is, when they've finished it half an hour ago. Losing a sense of time, leading to frequent missed appointments, may occur. A worrying sign is when we stop being able to do things we have done many times before. Seasoned card players who can no longer remember the cards that have been played are a cause for concern. No longer reading fiction because one can't keep track of the characters in a novel may be the first signs of a dementing illness. As well as memory and attention, behaviour may change in a variety of ways. Conversation may become more uninhibited, or the reverse may occur with increased withdrawal. Poor concentration and lack of interest in things that have previously been engaging are common. People may just become different from their 'old selves.'

As the illness progresses, (and dementia is always progressive though it may be very slowly progressive), more serious problems arise. People may get lost even in a familiar neighbourhood. They regularly forget the names of even close family and friends. They have difficulty not only in expressing themselves but in understanding what is said to them. They cannot perform simple household tasks such as cleaning and cooking that they have previously managed perfectly well. Time sense is further lost with difficulties in telling day from night. There may be more serious behaviour problems such as apparently unprovoked aggression. Extreme restlessness makes it sometimes necessary, (as was the case with the late French friend described in Chapter 6), to have someone with the person with dementia the whole time except when they are asleep.

Loss of short-term memory, of the capacity to remember what has just happened, is an explanation for the fact that, as their dementia advances, people with this condition may find it incredibly difficult to make choices. So, for example, one or two of our friends, faced with a restaurant menu, have taken half an hour or longer to decide what they want to eat. If you immediately forget what you've read as soon as you've read it, then it becomes impossible to keep in mind at the same time two, let alone three or four possible choices. People with this problem may be reluctant to allow others to choose for them, but, if they allow it, this may be the best solution.

Then, in the more advanced stages of dementia, people gradually become more dependent on others and need help with dressing, washing, feeding themselves. They may lose the power of speech, becoming incapable of expressing themselves at all. Our six friends who had dementia for at least several months and often for some years before they died all passed through these stages of dementia, finishing up very severely disabled. They all began with mild memory loss which was put down to a normal ageing process but then gradually deteriorated over a period of one to two years until it became obvious to their family members that there was something more seriously wrong. It was, however, only infrequently recognised by my friends themselves. For example, Jonathan Miller's son, William, described in a radio programme his father's deterioration. His mother had died of Alzheimer's in her fifties. He, Jonathan, had been the first President of the Alzheimer's Society, but resolutely refused to agree that he had dementia even when it was clearly put to him that indeed he had by a psychiatrist for the elderly. He would readily agree that his memory was faulty but refused to accept that he had dementia. In the end, a refusal to accept a diagnosis of dementia may not be a problem providing that the person accepts he or she has a serious memory problem.

Although it is most common in elderly people and the risk of dementia increases with age, it is *not* part of normal ageing. Only about one in twenty people over 65 has dementia and about one if five over 80. So, even over 80, four out of five people do *not* have dementia. The brain changes that are specific to dementia are not seen in most old people. It is, as we have seen, a progressive disease; those who have it gradually deteriorate from mild memory loss to lack of the ability to recognise their closest family members.

Types of dementia

There are many types of dementia, of which Alzheimer's Disease is the most common. This follows the pattern described above and was the type of dementia affecting most of my friends with the condition. Next most frequent is vascular dementia, which is notable because, unlike in Alzheimer's, as the disease progresses, there are periods, which may last months, when the individual returns to normal or near normal before relapsing again and showing further deterioration. This type of dementia is often accompanied by other signs of disease of the arteries to the brain, such as little strokes or transient ischaemic attacks (TIAs). Cognitive deficits are often patchy. For example, for the last six years of his life, the one friend I had who suffered from vascular dementia, had virtually no sense of direction and, on a number of occasions wandered out of the apartment in which he and his wife lived and then couldn't find his way home. Yet he was able to have a reasonably normal conversation about what he would like at his next meal until virtually the day he died. A much less common disorder is Lewy Body dementia, so-called because of the appearance of clumps of protein in the brain. As well as memory loss and confusion, in this type of dementia there may be Parkinson-like disorders of movement and visual hallucinations. There may be outbursts of aggressive behaviour. This is the type of dementia that is most likely to present problems in 'going gentle'.

Other types of dementia are much less common. As well as the memory loss, a significant number of people with dementia show difficult behaviour problems, for example, wandering off without knowing where they are going, becoming aggressive to family members and others caring for them, or showing lack of normal sexual inhibitions.

Diagnosis

If someone appears to be showing the first signs of dementia, a diagnostic assessment is highly desirable for a variety of reasons. For those worried they might have dementia but, in reality, are showing no more than the minor changes that come with ageing, it can be immensely reassuring to be given the all-clear. Those who are told they do have clear signs of dementia can start to plan their future lives while they still have sufficient cognitive abilities to do so. If they have not already done so, it is at this point before they lose mental competence that people need to make sure they have made their wills, completed an Advance Directive and registered one or possibly two Powers of Attorney, one for finance and the other for health and welfare (see Chapter 9 for further details). In a minority of people, memory loss can occur for reasons other than dementia. A diagnostic assessment will clarify the reasons for memory loss. For example, depression sometimes causes people to lose concentration with the development of a kind of 'pseudo-dementia'. Depression, unlike dementia. can be successfully treated. A general practitioner or hospital specialist will usually be able to distinguish between dementia and depression, but this may be difficult, especially if both are present. Very, very occasionally, a treatable cause of memory loss may be found such as an operable brain tumour.

Anyone suspected of having dementia should be referred to a memory service if one is available locally. Where the diagnosis is in doubt or the person involved is relatively young, under 65, then referral to a memory clinic or a hospital department of neurology or psychiatry so that a full clinical assessment and relevant investigations can be carried out is really necessary. In most cases this will include a brain scan. It is important to recognise that dementia cannot be diagnosed with a brain scan alone. This can only provide supportive information. People can have clearly abnormal brain scans with obvious brain shrinkage and yet show no or few signs of cognitive or intellectual deterioration.

They do not have dementia. Alternatively, quite advanced dementia can, unusually, be accompanied by a normal scan. Dementia is a diagnosis made by taking a history and clinical examination; investigations can only provide supplementary information.

About ten years before he died in 2019, as described in the radio programme mentioned above that was made by his son, William, Jonathan Miller's wife noticed his fabulous memory was not as good as it had been, and his famed eloquence was beginning to fade. The programme revealed the dramatic extent of his deterioration before he died. He no longer remembered he was married and showed disbelief when his son told him he was indeed married to Rachel, his wife of more than 60 years, who was in the room at the time. 'I've never been married,' he claimed. By the time he died, to use one of his own vivid analogies he had used many years previously, his mind, which had been like a fully furnished house, was empty. His existence was no more than 'an enforced tenancy in derelict premises.' His death, when eventually it mercifully came, was no more than a departure from a place that no longer existed. Losing all sense of time is linked to memory loss.

Another friend once turned up at our house on Christmas Eve at about half past midnight. She had been invited by another of our friends to lunch at midday and had lost all sense of day and night. She thought it was half-past midday. Finding her hostess did not answer her doorbell, she did remember that we lived close by, so she rang ours. We gave her a cup of tea and then I drove her back home about two miles away. As we arrived, she remarked on how empty the streets were and how unsurprising that was given, as she now realised, the time of night.

Dementia is often a problem linked to others

Only unusually is dementia an isolated health problem. One of my other friends became progressively weaker in his seventies from an inherited form of muscular dystrophy which had been present for over fifty years. His loss of memory became apparent about five years before he died and was far more distressing than his gradually increasing immobility. One friend with dementia developed a deep vein thrombosis following a fall and it was his leg problem which proved the most troublesome to him. Another friend, alongside or perhaps as part of her dementia, became quite paranoid and irrationally angry with her most supportive friends. This meant she spent her last years far more alone than she need have been. In the year before she died, she lost some of these paranoid ideas but a lot of the damage to her relationships had been done. One friend with dementia became so restless she could no longer be looked after at home and had to be placed in a residential care home. She was the only one of our friends who spent a significant amount of time in residential care.

Problems of communication

Inevitably, it is more difficult to communicate with someone whose memory and understanding is limited.

For the last three years of his life, a late friend recognised me as someone he knew but he did not have the vaguest idea who I was. This meant we could not have conversations about the past, which included a weekly game of squash followed by a chat over a beer for over twenty years. He had no idea he had ever played squash with anyone. This deprived us of the possibility of what we would have regarded as amusing, shared reminiscences. There was the time when he failed get out of the way of a ball I had hit. This resulted in our having to go to a local hospital accident and emergency department so that he could have a couple of stitches for a cut just above his eye. I would also like to have reminded him how competitive he was on the squash court, in contrast to his much more relaxed approach to his professional life. We generally played three games and almost invariably he would beat me in all three games or by two to one. Occasionally however the game finished up two to one in my favour. When this happened, he had an annoying habit of insisting on another game which, of course, he always won.

Effect of dementia on relationships

As one wife of a friend with advanced dementia put it: 'You can have a relationship with someone who has no memory, but it isn't a proper relationship' based on shared memories. As Jonathan's son put it, it's our memories that make each of us unique. Loss of memory means loss of individuality. Relationships may be limited to the comfort of a touch. Alan Bennett, the playwright, described how when he visited Jonathan, his old friend, the only way he could communicate with him was to hold his hand, a gesture which, as he rightly said, would have appalled Jonathan if he had been in his right mind.

Diversion and escape from boredom

For people with dementia, filling the empty spaces between meal-times and sleep is often a problem. One of my friends had been a talented artist who had spent many happy hours after her retirement and before the onset of her dementia in sketching on Hampstead Heath and attending art classes. Unfortunately, with the onset of dementia, she lost the skill she had had and became completely unable to paint or draw. This made it much more difficult to keep her occupied. In contrast, some of our friends with dementia developed new artistic activities. Another friend took up finger painting, an activity he particularly enjoyed sharing with his young grandchildren, as did they. The paintings they produced between them were highly colourful and attractive. Before he developed dementia, Jonathan Miller had developed an interest in a variety of artistic activities, sculpting in metal and producing patterns of coloured wooden blocks or paper he stuck onto boards. As his dementia advanced, he continued to create paper collages. Six years before he died, in 2013, Jonathan had an exhibition of his 'assemblages' at the Cross Street Gallery in Islington.

Treatment and outcome of dementia.

At the present time, there are no cures for any of the forms of dementia and the medication that is available has limited, though sometimes definite benefit and, not infrequently, unpleasant side-effects. For a few people it temporarily slows down the disease process. Although all my friends who suffered from dementia were given medication to relieve their symptoms, in none did it appear to make any really substantial difference. Most regarded medication as having doubtful benefit. On average, my friends who developed dementia lived about six years after their disease reached an advanced stage. But the condition may last much longer than this. I noticed clear signs of dementia in one of my predecessors at Great Ormond Street Children's Hospital, London, when she was 70. We were walking in the hospital car park when a man passed whose name she thought she ought to know but could not remember. I reassured her that he had arrived after she left the hospital. There was no reason why she should remember him. 'No', she said, 'I remember his name now. It's Philip Graham.' She died in a nursing home aged 95, twenty-five years later. The illness is usually shorter in people who develop the condition at a younger age. Jonathan Miller's mother who also had dementia, died at 55 only three or four years after first showing symptoms.

Quality of life in the advanced stages of dementia

All of the surviving family members of our friends who suffered from dementia agreed that both their own quality of life and that of the friend who had died was poor over this last period of their lives. Further, they all, apart possibly for the one with vascular dementia, agreed that their spouse, parent etc. would have preferred to have died earlier rather than experience their years with advanced dementia. In none of them was any attempt made to find health care assistance to end their lives; in any case, this would have been against the law. All the same, all their surviving family members thought that, had this been possible, an assisted death would have had the potential to ensure a better end to life. The issue of assisted dying in dementia is discussed further in Chapter 8.

Ways people with dementia can help themselves

There comes a point when it becomes obvious to family members that their father/mother/brother/sister etc is not just showing signs of normal ageing but that something much more serious is happening. Usually, it is some aspect of memory loss such as asking what time it is only a few minutes after having been told. It might be getting lost only a few hundred yards from home. With all my friends, the realisation came later, often much later to the person with dementia than it did to their family members.

At this point, it becomes essential for the person with early dementia to take steps to remind themselves of facts they will otherwise forget. Keeping a diary is helpful as is putting labels on doors and drawers to remind you of where things are kept. It is a good idea to have a list of telephone numbers by the landline or up to date contact details on your mobile. Try to put things like keys or your regular medication always in the same place so that you don't have to look for them every time you need them. Tell your family that you do not mind being reminded of things when it looks as if you have forgotten them.

A number of voluntary organisations provide information and facilities for people with dementia and their carers. In the UK, the Alzheimer's Society and Age Concern have helplines that can direct you towards invaluable help. There may be groups for people with dementia and/or their carers in your locality. A small number of the carers of my friends who had dementia attended such a group and one, in particular, found the experience invaluable. People with dementia and their carers should try and find out if there is such a group in their neighbourhood so that they can join it and share experiences with others and learn from theirs. It is not surprising that people with dementia are at risk of becoming depressed. Joining a group will mean that you can learn how other people have coped with an extremely frightening and indeed depressing future. All this presupposes that there has been an assessment with acceptance of the diagnosis of dementia. Denial of the diagnosis makes it much, much more difficult for others to help. Sadly, denial happened frequently among my friends and is very common.

All my friends with dementia had retired or given up their regular salaried jobs before they developed dementia though some were involved in voluntary work that they had to give up when their memories began to fail them. It is wise for people with dementia to tell those with whom they are working either in paid employment or voluntarily that they are having problems with their memory and ask them to be sure to let them know if they think they should be giving up. Stopping driving was especially hard for some of my friends but is essential if one is to avoid the possibility of a serious accident. The last thing one wants after a long, accident-free driving life is to injure a pedestrian. If you feel unsafe driving, you should give up at once, but if you are unsure, you can arrange a driving assessment at reasonable cost from an organisation like the Institute of Advanced Motoring. This involves having an experienced driver, usually a retired policeman, sitting next to you for an hour of so while you drive. This is not a pass or fail test, but your assessor will tell you after the drive whether he or she thinks you are safe to continue driving. (I have had one of these assessments every three years since I reached 80). If you have a diagnosis of dementia, you must inform the Driver and Vehicle Licensing Agency (DVLA). They may revoke your license or ask you to take a test before making a decision. Similarly, you shouldn't be cooking if you forget to turn the gas or electricity off when you've finished. If you carry on, you are putting others as well as yourself at risk. One of my late friends, who may have been showing signs of mild memory loss beforehand became more forgetful than she had been. At 93, she forgot to turn off the hob, filled her flat with smoke and nearly set it on fire when she left the gas on.

In the early and middle stages of dementia, it is still possible to lead an enjoyable life. As we have seen, taking up new activities such as drawing or painting, singing in a choir or going to concerts will all enhance your quality of life. In my mid-eighties, I participated as an 'able-bodied' volunteer at a local choir for people with Parkinson's disease, some of whom had mild to moderate dementia. One of my friends greatly enjoyed jazz and accompanied by his son, loved going to jazz concerts until quite late on in his dementing illness.

But there are also hazards for people at this stage of the condition. Going into unfamiliar situations is particularly likely to lead to an increase in confusion. This means that going into hospital for any reason puts a person with dementia at risk of serious disorientation. To reduce this risk, if a person with dementia really has to be admitted to hospital, they should always be accompanied by a friend or relative who can be with them, if at all possible, all the time. Otherwise, it is unlikely he or she will be able to find the toilet and the way back to bed without help. If the hospital has rules for visitors that make this impossible, you should protest by pointing to the web site for 'John's Campaign', which was set up to ensure that people with dementia could always have someone with them if they were admitted to hospital. Similarly, a person with dementia is at risk of increasing confusion if they develop an infectious illness such as a urinary tract infection or 'flu. For conditions caused by bacteria, then the early use of antibiotics will reduce the period of disorientation. On the other hand, some people who develop dementia have stipulated in an Advance Directive made when they were competent, that they would not wish to be given antibiotics for an infectious illness if they were in a state of advanced dementia. Such wishes should be respected.

Family carers of people with dementia

Because my interview with the family member focused on the person with dementia rather than on the carer, I did not obtain information systematically about the impact of looking after a person with dementia. There are, however, a large number of studies examining this issue. Some carers, especially if they are partners or spouses, will be of an age when they are at risk of developing dementia themselves. When one of my friends developed dementia, it was not long before her husband became affected with dementia himself. She died in 2015 but, at the time of writing in 2022, her husband is in residential care, as it was impossible for him to be looked after at home because he was so confused and disorientated.

Carers of people with dementia, whatever their age, are at significantly increased risk of developing depression. If the person with dementia also suffers from a terminal illness, as was the case with all the friends described here, the stress on the carer may become overwhelming. Looking after someone with dementia and a terminal illness inevitably means the carer has an extremely limited social life and suffers from loneliness. Looking after someone who is increasingly helpless is extremely exhausting. As well as depression, emotional reactions such as anger and crippling anxiety are common. Joining a group for relatives of people with dementia may provide you with tips to help ease the burden of caring. As I've already indicated, the Alzheimer Society and Age Concern are excellent sources of support. Their helplines and websites are useful sources of information and, in many parts of the country they run local groups for people with dementia as well as for their carers. The niece of one of my friends with dementia found attendance at one such group very helpful.

Even if it is time-consuming and irritating, a carer should ensure that the person with dementia retains as much independence as possible. It may take ages for them to do their buttons up, but they need to feel they can continue to do this themselves for as long as possible. Incontinence problems may be reduced if you make sure the toilet is easy to find and limit the intake of fluid before bedtime. Establishing a routine around washing and bathing will be helpful. It may be possible for your local Social Services Department to provide help a number of times a day with washing and dressing. (See Chapter 4 for information about the possibility of receiving financial help to pay for more substantial care).

There is a temptation for carers to ask questions of the person with dementia to see just how good or bad their memory is. Testing memory in this way is not a good idea; it is humiliating for the person being tested. You can get a good idea of someone's memory by showing photographs of people or places they have known in the past and getting the person with dementia to talk about them.

As the disease progresses, carers who can't leave the person with dementia alone as it's unsafe will need help with housework and shopping. When the person with dementia needs help with washing, dressing, and toileting, this need for assistance increases, sometimes quite rapidly. Other family members or friends may be able to step up but if that is not possible, social services may be able to assist. If, as may well be the case, such help is inadequate, you are going to need to buy in help. The internet will probably be a carer's main source of information how to find help, though personal recommendations are more reliable. It is natural that you should not wish to spend money in this way but think again. You have been saving for a rainy day, and now is the rainy day! Looking after someone who is dependent is incredibly tiring, so you should make every effort to have at least an evening a week and, every so often, a few days off. You also need people you can talk to and confide in; your situation is inevitably deeply stressful, and you will almost certainly need to unburden.

The decision whether to move someone with advanced dementia into a care home is always difficult. With people who live alone and become incapable of looking after themselves, there is no option, unless there is sufficient money to pay for twenty-four hour care and enough room to accommodate the carers. With others, emotional and financial factors enter into the equation as well as whether a suitable place is actually available. Only one of my friends with dementia went into a care home; with the rest it was feasible for home care to be provided. Short periods of admission to a care home to provide respite for the carer will allow a carer time to 'recharge' their batteries before resuming their caring tasks. One problem with respite admissions, however, is the risk that the person with dementia will suffer an increase in confusion which may make them unmanageable and lead to a breakdown in the respite arrangement. For this reason, it is often a better idea for a carer to employ a substitute carer, hopefully someone with whom the person with dementia is familiar, to live in their own home while they go away somewhere to recuperate.

Whether a person with dementia moves into a care home or paid care is employed in the home, care is expensive. For help and advice on placement and how care is funded, it is a good idea to contact the local Social Services Department, often via a helpline. This will provide an assessment of your needs and of your finances. In the UK, at the time of writing, if you have assets worth over £23,500 you pay for your own care.

Experiencing moderate or severe dementia at the end of life has more devastating effects than any other condition on the quality of life not only of the person affected but also of their partner and children. The lack of a cure does not mean that nothing can be done to improve life; indeed, I have suggested a number of measures which can reduce the impact of the illness and doubtless there are many others. Some talk or write about reframing the lives of people with dementia by using phrases such as 'living positively with dementia'. While these may be helpful to some, they cannot disguise the fact that people with this condition have had one of their most precious assets, their memory of the past, stolen from them. As I have already stated, all the relatives of those of my friends who died after a period of moderate or severe dementia agreed that their partner or parent would have preferred not to live through this period of their lives. At the present time, an assisted death is not possible in the UK even for those who are mentally competent so it will be many years before an assisted death becomes a possibility for people with dementia who have expressed a wish for this to happen before their illness has occurred. As we shall see in Chapter 8, my late friend, the moral philosopher, Mary Warnock, advocated for a change in the law along these lines but the public is not ready for such a move. As the number of people brought into personal contact with end-of-life dementia increases, this situation may change.

CHAPTER 8

Choosing the time you die

Introduction

For most of my friends, the timing of their deaths was largely outside their control. This was certainly the case for one of them, who died suddenly and unexpectedly from one moment to the next. Some of our other friends lost a long battle lasting years against the inexorable advance of a progressive disease. Others had a shorter terminal illness lasting only a few weeks or months. For a small number who all suffered a terminal illness which was going to end their lives in a few days or weeks, there came a point when their symptoms became so distressing, they decided they had had enough of life, abandoned the idea of a cure and opted for palliative care. They decided at this point to go as gentle as possible.

Taking Active Steps To End One's Life

The rate of suicide is twice as high in people with terminal illness as it is for other people of the same age in the general population. This is one way of making sure one controls the time of one's death but in fact, none of my friends made this choice. However, one did take active steps to die at the time he did. Three years before his death at the age of eighty-three, one friend began to suffer from a vascular form of Parkinson's Disease. This had possibly been brought on by exposure to organophosphates, a chemical which, as a farmer, he had frequently used in dipping sheep. To begin with the only noticeable features were a slight reduction in energy, difficulties in getting his words out and a slight tremor of his hands. These symptoms very slowly worsened over two years and then, in the last year of his life, very rapidly progressed. He had a number of little strokes. In the last few months, he also developed urinary problems which led to an operation on his prostate gland. He recovered well from the operation but then began to experience problems with his balance. This, combined with loss of power in his muscles, led to a number of falls. At the same time, he began to experience loss of vision due to macular degeneration. His hearing became impaired. It became harder for him to watch the television or do sudoku which he had previously enjoyed.

About six months before he died, he told his wife and his three sons that if he became unable to get out of bed, he would stop eating and drinking until he died. Six weeks before he died, a chair lift was installed to enable him to sleep upstairs in his own bed. Then, one day, in early January 2018, he found he could not walk at all. The family doctor suggested he should be admitted to a nursing home. He turned down this suggestion. At this point, he announced to his wife and his three sons that he did not want to live anymore and henceforth would stop eating and drinking. He asked to see his five grandchildren, then all in their late teens or early twenties, and, when they arrived, said to them 'I am going to show you how to die.' There might have been aspects of his earlier life which led him to this course of action. He had always been a man finding particular enjoyment in physical activity, unusually competent with his hands. The loss of his physicality was probably particularly distressing for him. Further, he had had to 'put down' a number of his animal stock as well as domestic pets because they were sick, and it seemed only humane to put them out of their misery. He applied the same logic to himself. His sons had a clear memory of a time when they were with their father and saw a man being pushed by his wife in a wheelchair. Their father had told them rather dramatically in words they did not forget, that if ever he was in this man's situation, they should take an axe to him and end his life.

While he was deteriorating, our friend took advice from a number of people, including me, as to ways he could shorten his life if this was what he wanted to do. I remember very clearly sitting on a bench with him outside his farmhouse looking out over the beautiful Herefordshire hills discussing the matter with him and explaining that assisted dying was not legal in the UK. His wife and sons were involved in his decision to stop eating and drinking and went along with it. He wrote an Advance Decision to Refuse Treatment and completed an advance statement, which he obtained from the charity Compassion in Dying. In these he made it clear that he did not want to receive treatment that would prolong his life, or for anyone to attempt to dissuade him from his course of action. He did continue to drink small amounts of water through a straw and his wife kept his lips and mouth moist with cream. He passed the time listening to classical music and liked to have books read to him. *Black Beauty* was a great favourite.

For the last six weeks he had regular, daily visits from a palliative care nurse, first provided privately but then, at the request of his GP, by the NHS, from St. Michael's Hospice near Hereford. Generally, the care they provided was excellent though one or two did try to encourage his wife to give him just a little to eat and this was not helpful. At no time did he waver in his determination to allow his death to happen. He made it easier for those around him by his complete acceptance of the situation. He felt in control of what was happening, and this is what he would always have wanted. A GP from his practice visited about every three days to provide further advice. His own GP was very supportive throughout but made it clear there was nothing he could do to hasten death. His doctor expressed the view that the time would surely come in the UK when this would be possible, but that time had not arrived. There was only one occasion when the health professionals faltered. He developed retention of urine and needed catheterisation. The palliative care team were not happy to do this themselves, so his GP was informed and arranged to do it himself.

Naturally, this was a very distressing time for his wife. She found it very painful not to be able to prepare meals for him and to eat with him. **But** one or other of their three sons arranged to spend the night in the house on all except one occasion so she was rarely alone. Some friends, including a couple who were both retired GPs, gave helpful support. The father of one of these GPs had taken the same course to bring about his own death. Other friends, who were alerted to the situation also came to visit.

Although he did not suffer significant pain, over the following two and a half weeks, our friend gradually became weaker until he started to become periodically drowsy and then slipped into and out of coma. About five days before he died, when he started to become agitated. It became possible for him to be prescribed morphine and this settled him. About three days before he died, he lapsed into a permanent coma with a marked death rattle, distressing for his family to hear. Just before he died, the palliative care nurse who was in attendance called in his wife and two of their sons, so they were present at the time of his death.

The day after he died the GP rang his wife to tell her there would have to be an inquest. She heard no more about this, and the GP told her this was because the Advanced Decision form had been signed. In any case, his wife was not subject to any police enquiries. She and their sons felt that their husband/father had experienced what they did not hesitate to call a 'good death'. In particular, they felt that he had been given a sense of purpose by the manner of his death and that they themselves had a real sense of 'doing it together' with him. He and they wanted him to 'go gentle' and this is what they achieved.

The manner of his death brings to the fore the need for a law in the UK which would enable mentally competent people who are terminally ill to have the assistance of a health professional to end their lives (see below). His wife and sons were clear it would have been beneficial to them if such a law had existed. It is not necessarily that he would have opted for such a death, but they were sure he would have put himself forward as a candidate for an assisted death. This would have meant that he had the reassurance of an assisted death if he desired one. It would also have put his GP and the palliative care nurses in a better place if their actions had ever been questioned.

For about the last six weeks of his life, another of my friends, who died of an abdominal cancer, suffered extreme discomfort from the swelling of his abdomen and a fracture of his spine caused by a fall in the toilet. He asked to be taken to Switzerland for an assisted death, but he was far too ill to travel. When I visited him two or three weeks before he died, he said: 'Philip, as you know I've always been opposed to you taking part in the campaign for legalising assisted dying. But I've changed my mind. You are right. That is what I would have wanted for myself.' Nursed in an excellent hospital, his pain and discomfort gradually worsened in the days before he died. His wife was with him for the whole of the last three weeks of his life and held his hand, as he had wished, for the last twenty-four hours.

Despite the fact that he was on a morphine drip, she described his last hours as 'agonising to watch'. He seemed in great distress, but it was impossible to tell if he was conscious or not. Eventually, to her relief, his breathing stopped. The absence of a law on assisted dying meant that he did not 'go gentle' as he wished.

Assisted dying

It is well known that, for many years, physicians have been prepared to accede to requests from their patients with a distressing terminal illness to end their lives, especially by giving large doses of morphine. In September 1939, Sigmund Freud, who had suffered severe pain from a cancer of the mouth for some years, reminded his physician that he had promised to end his life if the pain became unendurable. He told him this was now the case and asked for help. By the following morning he was dead. The doctor's behaviour was illegal then and remains so now. Doctors are naturally unwilling to engage in such illegal activity, though there are many who rely on the principle of 'double effect'. Doctors are permitted to give pain-relieving medication even if this will shorten the patient's life. They are not allowed to give more than would ease pain and suffering. During the second half of the twentieth century a movement grew, in the UK as well as elsewhere, to legalise assisted dying.

In 1994, the State of Oregon passed the Death with Dignity Act which took effect in 1997. This allowed mentally competent patients who were suffering from a terminal illness and likely to die within six months to request help from a health professional to end their own lives at a time of their choosing. Before the request is approved, the patient must make both an oral and a written application. If there is the possibility of a mental illness, the patient must be referred to a counsellor for an opinion as to whether there are mental health issues that might be influencing the request. In the twenty-five years this law has been in operation, it has worked smoothly. A relatively small number of requests are received. In Canada, where there is now similar legislation in place, about 3% of deaths are preceded by a request for an assisted death but only about two-thirds of those whose request is approved, actually act on it.

In recent years, a number of other American states, California, Colorado, Hawaii, Maine, New Jersey, New Mexico, Vermont, and Washington—as well as Washington, DC have passed similar legislation. All the Australian states have followed suit. Since 2001, voluntary euthanasia, in which a doctor can end a patient's life or request, has been operating in the Netherlands. Similar legislation to the Netherlands is now operating in Belgium, Luxembourg, Spain and Canada. The only country which allows foreign nationals to request a health professional assisted death is Switzerland where a number of organisations of which the best known is Dignitas provides this service for people from abroad. On average, about one person a week travels to Switzerland from the UK for this purpose. None of our friends took this step though, as we have seen, our friend who stopped eating and drinking took the matter into his own hands. At least one other friend discussed the possibility of an assisted death. She was much taken by the example of one of her close friends, a lifelong campaigner for the right to die, who stopped eating and drinking at the age of 86, dying in October 2014, three months before our friend. Further, a number of the other family members I interviewed felt that the last few weeks or months of the lives of their terminally ill relatives were of such poor quality that, if the option of an assisted death at home had been open to them, they might just have taken it.

At the time of writing, mid-2023, members of the UK and the Scottish parliaments are actively considering the possibility of new legislation to make an assisted death possible. The proposal that is finding most favour at the present time is based on the Oregon model but will provide an additional safeguard. It would allow someone who was terminally ill with less than six months to go before their predicted death, was mentally competent and had formed a persistent wish to die, to be able to apply for an assisted death. Assistance would be provided by a health professional, but the person would be responsible for taking the lethal medication themselves. Before their application for an assisted death was approved, legislation recently discussed in Westminster has included the proposal that the case would be considered by a judge who would have to check they were not being coerced into this decision and that the other conditions for an assisted death were met.

The arguments in favour of a change in the law in this direction are compelling. If someone who is terminally ill, is suffering intolerably and is mentally competent to make the decision, it contravenes the principle of patient autonomy, the right patients have to make decisions concerning their own health care, not to have the possibility of an assisted death. Once patients have made a successful request, they may or may not decide to go ahead with it; about half do and the other half do not. But in any event, they have the reassurance of knowing that if at any time they wish to die they can activate the process. They are significantly more in control. A further reason for changing the law is that the existing legal position is unsafe, even harmful. The absence of a law means, as we have seen, that people take matters into their own hands and die by suicide. The rates of suicide and attempted suicide in the terminally ill are about twice the expected rate for people of the same age. A number of people who try to take their own lives fail to do so and not infrequently harm themselves in the process. Family members who assist their relatives to die or to attempt to die face the possibility of prosecution or at least lengthy interrogation by the police, although assisting someone to stop eating and drinking is legal. The wife of our friend who ended his life by stopping eating and drinking was lucky to have a supportive GP and not to face questioning by the police. But did our friend really need to have to go through a period of increasing starvation before he died?

Having control over the timing of one's death in this way would allow the terminally ill person to have the opportunity to say goodbye in one's own time. For both patients and their relatives this makes possible a more emotionally satisfying end to a life. Finally, there is very considerable public support in the UK for the proposed new law. Population surveys over the last three decades have revealed a gradually increasing level of support which is now running at around 75-80%. It is of particular interest that people with disabilities support such legislation at about the same level or even higher (86%). Further, medical organisations such as the British Medical Association and the Royal College of Physicians that until recently showed opposition, have all now adopted a neutral stance. The only group of doctors remaining opposed as a group though there are numerous exceptions, are palliative care physicians. The palliative care movement and the establishment of hospices owes everything to the pioneering work of Dame Cicely Saunters, a committed Christian. Though many palliative care specialists these days are not motivated by Christian faith, the movement, which has been responsible for major improvements in the care of the terminally ill, retains a strong Christian ethos associated with belief in the sanctity of the human body and the view that only God has the right to decide when we should die.

The arguments against such a new law do have to be seriously considered. In UK parliamentary debates, one of the most commonly expressed objections is that the integrity of the body is sacrosanct. It is only divine providence that should determine when a person dies.

For atheists, of course, who do not believe in God, this argument does not hold. But even for those who believe in a divine presence, it is difficult to see how they can reconcile their acceptance of other forms of medical intervention which change the course of illness while rejecting help to end terminal suffering. None of the Abrahamic religions, Judaism, Christianity and Islam, are prepared to do other than condemn assisted dying. All the same, the leading organisation that campaigns for a change of legislation to allow assisted dying, has an affiliated group of interfaith leaders drawn from both reform Jewish and Christian groups which support its aims. Further, population surveys reveal that the great majority of people with faith support legislation for assisted dying.

A further argument against the introduction of a new law is that it would be expensive to administer and would take away resources that would be better spent on palliative care. It is certainly the case that palliative care is under-funded in the UK. Most hospices depend to a very considerable extent on charitable funding as well as funding from the NHS. However, the relatively small numbers of people with terminal illness who would avail themselves of the opportunity of an assisted death (less than 1% of all deaths), suggest the cost would be relatively insignificant. Further, all the evidence suggests that in jurisdictions that have introduced an assisted dying law, palliative care services have been more adequately funded than before the new legislation was introduced. This has been the case in Oregon, in Canada and probably most significantly in Australian states. Meanwhile, the UK government is at last beginning to accept that palliative care should not be dependent on charitable funding.

The idea that if assisted dying legislation were introduced, there would be a 'slippery slope' with new more permissive legislation rapidly following is given the lie by the fact that in Oregon, as well as in all other jurisdictions in which assisted dying is now the law, no such progression has occurred. The 'slippery slope' argument is relevant to a significant number of the laws we pass, whether these relate to family matters such as marriage, divorce and abortion as well as to vast amounts of legislation in other fields. It would not be possible to introduce speed limits on the roads, for example, if every time a 30 mph limit was put in place opponents insisted this would be followed by a 20 mph restriction.

Another objection relates to the possibility that greedy relatives would coerce their family members who were dying to request assisted deaths. All the evidence is to the contrary. Relatives generally try to dissuade their terminally ill family members from taking this route because they cannot bear to see them go. Not a single case of coercion has been revealed in Oregon where such legislation has been in place for twenty-five years. Further, in legislation currently proposed for the UK, it would be the responsibility of a judge as well as the independent doctors monitoring the cases to ensure such coercion did not occur. Ironically, those who raise the possibility of coercion bizarrely don't seem worried about the possibility of people being coerced into traveling to Dignitas or ending their own lives, both of which will continue to happen without safeguards if there isn't a change in the law.

My late friend, Mary Warnock, the moral philosopher, wrote a book *Easeful Death* jointly with an oncologist, Elisabeth Macdonald. In it she wrote on this issue:

> 'It is not difficult to imagine feeling that one's children were getting impatient either for their inheritance or simply for relief from the burden of care and that one had not so much a right to ask for death, as a duty to do so, now that it was lawful to provide it. There undoubtedly exist predatory or even exhausted relatives. But it is insulting to those who ask to be allowed to die to assume that they are incapable of making a genuinely independent choice, free from influence. (Indeed, there are people so determined to confound their children, if they see them as hovering over a hoped-for corpse, that their will to spite them by staying alive may outweigh their wish to escape their own pain).'

There is also a concern that people who are terminally ill, especially those living in expensive residential homes, will want to end their lives so that they can stop being a burden to their families. It is widely thought that it is the duty of family members to reassure their dying relatives that they are in no way being a burden.

They are loved and any expense is willingly given. As may be imagined, it is not so easy to persuade intelligent people facing a few months of dreadful quality of life that money is better spent on them than on, for example, the university fees of a grandchild. Again, Mary Warnock put the argument succinctly. She wrote:

'In any case, to ask for death for the sake of one's children or other close relatives can be seen as an admirable thing to do, not in the least indicative of undue pressure, or pressure of any kind. Other kinds of altruism are generally thought worthy of praise. Why should one not admire this final altruistic act? And it would not be wholly altruistic: the desire to avoid squandering resources, or being a burden is combined, in the cases we are considering, with a sense that prolonging life is both futile and painful. It is idle to try to separate these motives. Part of what makes a patient's suffering intolerable may be the sense that he is ruining other people's lives. If he feels this keenly, and asks to be allowed to die, he is not a vulnerable victim, but a rational moral agent'.

Assisted dying for people with dementia

As we have seen in Chapter 7, six of our friends who have recently died suffered from dementia for several months or, in most cases, for years before their end. In all but one of the cases, their surviving relatives felt that the quality of life of the terminally ill with dementia was extremely poor. All felt that the person with dementia would, if in their right minds, have preferred not to be alive while they could not even recognise the members of their families. The surviving relatives felt similarly. As one wife put it: 'You can have a conversation with someone with dementia, but it isn't the same.' Inability to share memories reduces the quality of a relationship to a point where it is hardly worth having.

The argument in favour of a law allowing people to stipulate in advance that they would like their lives to be ended if they develop advanced dementia is well illustrated by the story of the husband of one of my late friends whose death from heart disease and dementia is described in Chapter 7. Her husband, now 90, was a pioneer in developmental paediatrics as well as the founder of a successful poetry magazine he launched while at University. Sixty years later, it has only just stopped publication. This friend is now (February 2023) in a nursing home, where he has been for the last five years, slowly deteriorating in every way. He is now unable to speak and does not recognise his children when they visit. Having been washed, shaved and dressed, he sits in a chair all day unable to join in the various activities that are on offer. His sons are sure that if he had known he would reach this state, he would have wanted his life to be ended. As he eats so little and is losing weight, the home has put him on protein supplements. He could well live another three or four years.

The question therefore arises whether people, when mentally competent, ought to have the right to make advance decisions to the effect that if they become severely demented, they would like to have their lives terminated by euthanasia. This was Mary Warnock's view. She wrote: 'If you're demented, you're wasting people's lives – your family's lives – and you're wasting the resources of the National Health Service.' Most of those who advocate for a new law on assisted dying think it is important that the person requesting to die should be fully mentally competent at the time the final decision was made to go ahead. This is certainly the view of Professor Ray Tallis, a passionate advocate for assisted dying for the mentally competent, terminally ill patient who believes 'informed consent at the time a lethal medicine is taken is a totally necessary safeguard against abuse.'

Of course, in the early stages of dementia, a person would be competent to make this decision, but the expectation is that people with dementia would not wish to die until the disease had advanced to the point when, for example, they did not recognise their close family members. At this point they would not be mentally competent. Those who wish for sufferers with advanced dementia to be allowed to have their lives terminated therefore propose that people in the early stages can make advance directives stating that once their disease had progressed to a point when their quality of life was unacceptable, they could have their lives terminated.

Mary Warnock's view was that people who face a progressive form of dementia ought to be able to stipulate, in advance of the event, their wish to die. If they are not competent to make a decision themselves, their proxies should be able to decide on an assisted death on their behalf once they have reached an advanced stage of the condition. In the Netherlands, it is legal for doctors to end the lives of people with dementia, even if this is at an early stage, if they have previously expressed a wish for this to happen. Polling in the Netherlands suggests that about half the population support this position, but in other countries there is greater reluctance to extend assisted dying criteria to dementia sufferers. A majority want a right to make such a momentous decision for themselves, but not for others to make it for them. And amongst the medical profession even this limited position does not command support although there are signs that opinion amongst health professionals is beginning to change.

There are two main objections to the type of legislation currently applied in the Netherlands. The first is that expressed by the Alzheimer Society. Many people with dementia, it claims, enjoy a good quality of life and there is no reason why they should want their lives to end. Further, much can be done to alleviate the symptoms of dementia so what is needed is not a defeatist attitude but a positive approach. This point of view is, of course, valid for those at an early stage of the disease, but much more dubious, indeed Mary Warnock thought, ridiculous for those whose disease has progressed to the point at which they have lost the ability to communicate, need help with toileting and feeding and can no longer recognise their family members or friends.

A second objection can be described as pragmatic. In most countries, such as the UK where legislation on assisted dying is not in place, it is believed that the general public finds it abhorrent to suggest that people with dementia or other fatal illnesses should be able to end their lives because they feel they are a burden to their families and to society. People with dementia and other terminal illnesses, it is widely thought, should be reassured that their family members and society are happy to continue to look after them for as long as it takes. Many members of the House of Commons who took part in the 2015 debate on assisted dying held in September 2015 reported this was the view that had been frequently put to them by their constituents.

In an unpublished lecture titled 'Easeful Death for the Very Elderly' that Mary Warnock delivered to the Society of Old Age Rational Suicide (SOARS) in 2010 when she herself was eighty-six, she pointed to the neglect of the plight of people with dementia in discussions of assisted dying. It was widely argued that a health professional assisted death should not be permitted for people with advanced dementia because they could not give informed consent. Even if people had made Advance Directives asking for such a death if they became severely demented, they might have changed their minds. But, Mary argued, the concept of a change of mind was meaningless. 'The patient has no mind left to them to change, no settled intention, no powers to foresee the future or consider the course of a whole life.' This made it necessary for people with mild dementia to be able to make out an Advance Directive if they did not wish to continue to live once their condition had advanced to a point they themselves could define.

Mary viewed the protests of organisations such as the Alzheimer Society that people with advanced dementia can be happy and enjoy life to be offensive. She wrote: 'I simply do not want to think that, in the future, I may be patronised by people pretending to believe my fantasies ...' As for the argument that people should not be allowed to take their own lives because they feel a burden, Mary asked, as she had many times previously, why should 'altruism turn out to be the thing that is avoided?' at the end of life. For her this is a moral issue 'of personal integrity, of trying to behave consistently and trying, roughly speaking, to do what is right by other people' It is also a philosophical issue. 'Once the brain has reached a certain stage of tangles and degeneration which cannot be reversed, I believe I am not the same person as I was and I can take no further responsibility as a moral being.' She goes on to note that some people think it is wrong to take life no matter how deteriorated a person is. Mary recognized the strong resistance to the idea that advance directives should be honoured even in the cases of advanced dementia but, she writes 'I believe that society is moving in this direction.' Of course, as Mary rightly wrote, societal attitudes may change, as they clearly have in the Netherlands. Mary made herself very unpopular by advocating for assisted deaths for people with advanced dementia, yet, as I have said above. all the family members of those of our friends who died while in a state of severe dementia felt that the last months of their terminally ill relatives had not been worth living. It is important to add that no jurisdiction in the UK is currently considering the possibility of an assisted death for people with dementia who are not mentally competent. Nor is there any evidence that such legislation would meet with public approval. All the same, the issue is worthy of full discussion.

Conclusion

While legislation to enable people with advanced dementia to have an assisted death is clearly problematic, there is far less reason to question the need for such legislation for the mentally competent. One of the advantages of an assisted death is that, to some degree at least, it is possible for the terminally ill patient to choose the time of their demise. Thus, people who have a last wish, for example, to be around for the birth of a new grandchild or great grandchild may be able to do so. It is also easier to ensure that, if they wish it, close family members can be present in the last few hours to say their goodbyes. At the present time, it is neither easy nor cheap for UK citizens to organise an assisted death in Switzerland for themselves. Most who do so are middle-class, highly educated, at least reasonably affluent and are suffering from chronic, ultimately fatal neurological disorders. It is relatively easy to find out how to go about it by using the internet. It is against the law for family doctors to give advice on this matter, but most will provide the information required by Dignitas or whichever organisation terminally ill patients choose to use for this purpose, although not necessarily in the form they would prefer. The movement for change has progressed, not least in the medical profession.

CHAPTER 9

Practical Matters

Introduction

Dear Reader, I have no idea of your financial circumstances. You may be entirely dependent on the state pension. If you are, you will probably be sitting, hopefully in a comfortable chair, in a public library reading a borrowed copy. Or you may be immensely rich, perhaps sitting on your yacht in the Mediterranean gazing up from time to time to appreciate the infinite blue Much more likely than either of these, financially you are somewhere in between. Whatever the resources at your disposal, as a terminally ill person or as a family member of a terminally ill person, money, though probably not top of your list, is really something you should be thinking about.

Making a will

When you die, you will leave at least some possessions behind you. Even if you have nothing but the nightdress or pyjamas in which you take your last breath, you still have something to leave and, if you wish to have maximum say in what happens to your possessions, you will want to make a will. If you do not leave a will and die intestate, and you have a spouse or civil partner, he or she will inherit the first £270,000 of your estate but not necessarily everything else.

What follows is based on the assumption that you are getting on in years and have decided to make a will.

Do you need legal advice?

It is perfectly possible to make a will that is legally valid without the help of a solicitor. If you use a solicitor, you should enquire first as to the likely fees; they vary greatly. If you decide to write your own will, all you need is a computer and printer or legible handwriting, a clear idea of how you want to leave your possessions/assets, two witnesses who sign their names and give their addresses, and a dated document. Do make sure that at least two people know where your will is to be found after you die.

There are a number of reasons why you may need the advice and help of a solicitor in drafting your will, It is probably desirable to consult a professional if you:

- Own some property that you share
- Own a business
- Own a property or have other possessions or a bank account overseas
- You think there is even a whiff of a possibility that your will might be contested by a disappointed potential beneficiary, or

- You have reason to think your mental competence to make a will might be disputed.

Are you legally competent to make a will? To be legally competent, you must (i) understand the nature of the act and its effects; (ii) understand the extent (as distinct from value) of the property of which you are disposing; and (iii) understand and appreciate the claims that might be made on your estate. In other words, you must (i) understand what you are doing and its 'reach'/impact; (ii) recall what you have been told and your 'responsibilities'; (iii) be capable of weighing up what you have heard and apply this to your 'responsibilities' and (iv) be able to communicate your decision.

Many will be mildly insulted to think they might not be mentally competent to make a will but, particularly for those getting on in years, it is worth thinking about. You are regarded as competent if you have a clear idea of what you possess and of all those who might have a legitimate claim to be remembered in your will. For most of my readers, their competence will not be in question but if you have noticed some recent loss of memory or are beginning to have difficulty in making decisions or have seen your family doctor or a psychiatrist or a neurologist in recent years reporting any of these problems, it is wise to obtain written confirmation from a doctor that you are mentally competent at the time you make your will. The doctor will need to make sure that you understand what making a will involves and that you are not suffering from a mental disorder that might affect your judgement in making testamentary decisions. It should be added that, even if you are not legally competent to make a will, you may well have ideas how you wish your possessions to be distributed after your death and, if this is the case, it is sensible to let those who will be left behind know what these wishes are so that they can be taken into consideration.

Naming your executors

Executors are those people you name to manage your estate after you die. If you are leaving no more than a few hundred pounds, you may think it is ludicrous for what you leave to be termed your 'estate', but that is the legal term for it. If you have a spouse or partner and children all of whom get on well together, you may well nominate them and them alone as executors. Even in this case, you may think it sensible to add an outside person, perhaps someone with business experience who knows your family members, who can mediate if there unexpectedly turns out to be some dispute between your beneficiaries or those who have been excluded. (Some consider it is not a good idea to appoint a solicitor to be an executor as there might be a tension between their professional obligations and the position the family best might take).

How to decide who are going to be your beneficiaries?

If you have a spouse or partner of long-standing, you are likely to wish to leave all your possessions to them on the understanding that when, in their turn, they die, they are likely to have made a will which takes your wishes into account. If you do not have a partner but do have children, you will probably want to leave what you have to them, usually in equal measure. Some people who have already, in their lifetime, given money to one or more of their children but not to others, may wish to take what they have already given into account in deciding how much to leave to each child. An alternative which many find more attractive, is to give according to need during one's lifetime but to leave in equal measure after death regardless of how much has been given to each child beforehand. In distributing what you leave behind you will almost certainly wish to be fair but also to treat everyone equally. These two principles, fairness and equality, may be in conflict. This will be the case if your children are very different in their financial circumstances. In this situation, you might wish to explain to your children before you die why you have made the decisions you have.

You may wish to leave specific sums of money to particular people, for example to grandchildren, and the residue to your spouse/partner and/or children, as well as some money to charities. What you leave to charities is not subject to inheritance tax. You may also wish to leave specific gifts or particular possessions to other relatives and/or friends. If you deliberately omit people who might think they have a right to be mentioned, you need to think carefully. Some have a possible right to contest your will. Often, the only people to benefit from contested wills are lawyers.

After your death, the contents of your will are available to the public.

If you are going to leave behind a really substantial sum of money or properties, you may be encouraged by lawyers to create a trust or trusts perhaps with a view that subsequent generations can benefit from your wealth. Trusts are likely also to be on the table if, for example, your will says something like 'on the second death of a husband/wife/civil partner, I leave equally to my children but if any has predeceased me leaving children their share is to go to their children equally at age 21'. In these circumstances it is strongly advisable to receive professional input on the drafting of your will.

You should look at your will at least every three or four years and, where necessary, make out a new one. Alternatively, you can change it by adding what is called a codicil, a signed, dated and witnessed amendment to your will.

Lasting Power of Attorney (Property and Affairs)

Completing this document allows you to decide who you wish to manage your financial affairs if you are no longer competent to do so yourself. The person you choose is called your attorney and you will also need to choose a replacement attorney if, for some reason, your first choice becomes unavailable. A third party will need to certify you are competent at the time you complete the form.

Making out a Lasting Power of Attorney is definitely worth doing if you have been told there is a reasonable chance you may lose your mental competence. This may be the case if you are developing dementia or for some other reason. Of course, you may lose competence suddenly for some unpredictable reason, such as a serious accident or a stroke. If you are worried this may happen, then again you should complete a Lasting Power of Attorney. This needs to be registered with the Office of the Public Guardian for it to be valid. Remember the responsibility of your attorney is only activated if you lose mental competence. While you are competent, it is you who makes the financial decisions, signs the cheques or makes the bank transfers. On the other hand, if you lose competence and have not made out a Power of Attorney form, then someone will need to apply to the Court of Protection to manage your financial affairs or they may be put in the hands of the Office of the Public Guardian (()PG) This may work out well but will inevitably lead to more bureaucracy than would otherwise be the case.

Making out a Power of Attorney currently costs £82 to register, but you may choose to pay for legal advice to ensure the form is completed 'properly' with the input of a professional. There is great variation in how much solicitors charge so you may need to shop around if you do not have a personal recommendation. The OPG charges you and sends the form back if you have not filled it in to their satisfaction. Then you may have to pay again when you re-submit.

Advance Decisions

Most of my friends had completed an Advance Decision (also known as a Living Will) document before they died. Despite the fact this is a very simple, cost-free thing to do, only about one in five of the general population complete this document. In your living will, you are first asked to list the forms of medical treatment you do NOT consent to. For example, you are asked if you do not consent to medical treatment if you have 'an imminently life-threatening physical illness for which there is little or no hope of recovery (in the opinion of appropriately qualified doctors'). You are then asked if you DO consent to medical treatment in other circumstances, for example, if it is given 'to alleviate pain or distress aimed at my comfort. I maintain this request even in the event it may shorten my life.' You are then asked if you have any wishes in relation to any particular illnesses. You are then asked for the names of two people who you wish to take healthcare decisions on your behalf in case you cannot do so yourself. Finally, you are asked to give the names of two people (one of them should be your GP) with whom this advance directive has been deposited. The document has to be witnessed.

An advance directive is legally binding on doctors who are taking decisions with patients who are seriously ill. Indeed, any doctor wilfully ignoring a wish expressed in an advance directive could face legal action. This does not mean that decisions are always taken in compliance with a patient's wishes. What happens not infrequently is that the wishes expressed in the advance directive have not been brought to the attention of the doctor taking the decision. Most commonly the document is held by the GP and the decision is being made by a hospital doctor or by paramedics in an ambulance. In these cases, it is up to a relative to draw the attention of the doctor or paramedic to the wishes of the patient, if possible obtaining the document from the patient's filing system or the GP.

In fact, in none of the terminal illnesses of my friends was the advance decision document invoked to persuade a doctor that a course of action proposed needed to be reconsidered in the light of the preferences the terminally ill person had laid down. It could be argued, and indeed I would argue, that in a small number of cases where, at least in retrospect, life was prolonged by medical interventions beyond the point at which it was desirable to do so, it would have been better if the Advance Decision had been invoked. But, for whatever reason, this never happened. A not infrequent complication is that the patient has made a clear statement that treatment is not to be given in certain situations but one or more of the close relatives cannot bear the thought of their loved one dying and persuades the doctor to give a treatment to prolong life where this is against the wishes the patient has previously expressed. A doctor who complies with a relative's request is acting unlawfully but may well find the relative's request difficult to resist. Again, this situation did not arise in the terminal illnesses of any of my friends. A not uncommon situation arises when someone is taken seriously ill, perhaps appears to have died. An ambulance is called and the paramedics immediately embark on emergency life-saving treatment such as cardiopulmonary resuscitation (CPR). At this point, a husband or wife may remember that this is not what is wished for in the advanced directive. The paramedics say their instructions are to carry out CPR regardless. The relevant document cannot be found. The patient survives but is irreparably brain-damaged. One solution both for paramedics and for hospital doctors might be for each of us to carry the advance directive document on our mobile phone.

An Advance Decision form free to download is available from a number of sources. The simple one I have used is obtainable from Compassion in Dying (https://beta.compassionindying.org.uk/). This organisation also provides useful information on other end of life issues. There are more complicated advance directive forms available that take account of a variety of different scenarios but for nearly all purposes a simple form is quite adequate.

Lasting Power of Attorney: Personal Welfare.

This document authorises an appointed person to speak on behalf of a person who is not competent, for example to a nursing/residential home and, if necessary, make a complaint with legal status. Like the lasting power of attorney (Property and Affairs), this document enables you to choose who you would like to take decisions for you in the event of your not being competent to take them yourself, but in this case for decisions involving your health and personal welfare. The document is specifically designed to take account of situations where a doctor has to decide whether to give you life-prolonging treatment at a time when you are terminally ill and no longer expected to enjoy a reasonable quality of life. If you have made out an Advance Directive, you have given the names of two people who you wish to take decisions for you in this situation if you can't do this yourself. Bearing in mind the advance directive has legal standing and that consulting a solicitor to help you complete the rather complicated document and registering a lasting power of attorney with the Office of the Public Guardian will cost you money you may well feel it is unnecessary to go to the trouble of filling in the power of attorney form for health and welfare decisions.

Inheritance tax

This is both one of the fairest and the least popular of the taxes we pay. It's fair because it's a progressive tax only paid by the well-off. It's unpopular because people see it as stopping them from doing what they most want to do – passing on the wealth that they have earned and accumulated to their children. So strongly do wealthy people feel about inheritance tax that many of them manage to avoid paying the full effective rate applicable to their estate. Inheritance tax is paid on only about one in twenty estates. Given the value of property in London and south-east England, it is clear that a large number of people who have a lot to leave arrange their affairs so that no inheritance tax is paid after their deaths.

At the time of writing (June 2023), the standard inheritance tax rate in the UK is 40%. It's only charged on the part of your estate that's above the nil rate band threshold which at the moment is £325,000 that passes to someone other than your spouse, civil partner or a qualifying charity. In addition, there is the residential nil rate band of £175,000 meaning for a married couple/civil partners who own their home, on the second death up to a £1m of assets can pass free of inheritance tax if the recipient of the family home is a 'lineal descendant' and the aggregate estate of the second to die is less than £2m. The residential nil rate band tapers to zero if the aggregate estate of the second to die exceeds £2.35m. As a general rule, if you are the second spouse to die, your estate will need to pay 40% of any amount your estate is worth over £650,000 albeit it may be your estate will need to pay 40% of any amount your estate is worth over £1 million.

Inheritance tax is also payable on all gifts of more than £3,000 annually that you have made from your capital during the seven years before your death. The amount of tax tapers down so that if you die six years after you've made the gift, the tax is reduced from 40% to 8%. Further, gifts you make from your current income do not attract inheritance tax whatever the level of gift so long as it is part of a general pattern of giving and not a one -off payment. Your executors will, however, need to be able to demonstrate that your gifts have indeed come from income and not from capital and that the intention was for the gift to be repeated annually. If you are making such gifts from income, you should make sure to complete the last page of Form IHT403 each year. This states both your income and your expenditure under a number of headings. Your executors will need to complete this form after your death to substantiate to HMRC that the gifts 'qualify' and are thus outside inheritance tax; so do complete it.

The question arises whether you should take steps during your lifetime to reduce the amount of inheritance tax payable on your death. What is most important is not to leave yourself short and not to give away and then receive funds back from the gift recipient. HMRC has well-honed anti-avoidance rules to bring back within the donor's estate subject to Inheritance tax 'gifts with reservation of benefit' if the benefit is received at any time in the seven years preceding the death of the donor. There is also a stand alone tax called the Pre Owned Asset Tax.

As a rough guide, if you stand to leave an estate that is significantly likely to be within inheritance tax, especially if you have adequate pension provision, it may be worth asking a solicitor or accountant for advice on measures you might take to mitigate the likely Inheritance tax due on the second death. If you are going to leave less than this, then no matter how strongly you hate the idea of giving the Chancellor of Exchequer money to spend on armaments and bureaucracy, you should probably avoid spending sums of money on lawyers just to save relatively small amounts of tax.

Transferring skills and responsibilities before you die

One of the lessons from my interviews carried out with a surviving family member is the need for those who have a personal bank account, who pay the bills and make out the standing orders and direct debits to ensure that they make it easy for a survivor to take over these responsibilities. Paying all bills etc from a joint account will sort out this problem and save a lot of trouble later. Typically, a husband pays all the bills and then, when he dies, perhaps unexpectedly, the wife is left to manage without a clue what to do. Of course, the wife may undertake all these responsibilities in which case her husband needs to be able to take over if this becomes necessary. Sorting out these problems can be expensive, time-consuming and anxiety-provoking.

Similarly, if one of a couple takes responsibility for checking the amounts paid for gas and electricity, water, the alarm system and other regular payments for example to charities, then, in case of unexpected death, that person should make sure the other knows what to do to avoid mistakes over payments. Completing the annual tax return is also something that needs to be done jointly. If there is a query over the ability of the other person to have the competence to manage this, then the necessary skills need to be transferred to an adult child or other responsible person. For the same reason, if there are no complicating issues such as a previous marriage, it makes it much easier for a survivor if any property or investments such as stocks and shares are held in joint names. All this presupposes a degree of trust between the two members of a couple. Lack of trust will create unnecessary expense.

Coordinating care

Not all people who are terminally ill need extra help in the house before they die, but quite a number do. Reluctance to ask for or engage such help is a common mistake. Most of my friends who got help in said afterwards they wished they had done this sooner. There are a number of reasons why extra help may be needed: domestic tasks like cleaning, shopping, meeting dependency needs like dressing and feeding, cooking meals and respite care or enabling a carer to take time off. Some of these needs can be fairly easily met without getting extra help in, especially if there is a bit of extra money available. A relative, neighbour or friend may be available to do necessary shopping. Prepared meals can be bought to save on the cooking. Clothes can be bought that are easier to wear, T-shirts or slipovers rather than shirts or blouses with fiddly buttons, for example.

There may well come a point, however, when it is clear that extra help in the house is needed, to begin with just once or twice a week for part of the day, then every day for part of the day, then all day every day and finally twenty-four hour, seven day a week care. There is often great reluctance to accept the need for care. Expense and not wanting a stranger in the house are the two most common reasons given. As far as expense is concerned, you may be entitled to free care provided by your local social services department. The following web site provides information on what you can get for free.

https://www.nhs.uk/conditions/social-care-and-support-guide/care-services-equipment-and-care-homes/care-and-support-you-can-get-for-free/

You will see from this web site that you can get for free adaptations for your home, such as banisters for your stairs or a stair lift that cost less than £1,000 as well as help at home for a limited number of weeks after coming out of hospital. If you are very seriously incapacitated so that if you didn't get help at home you would have to be looked after in hospital, you are entitled to what is called 'NHS continuing healthcare' which will pay for a considerable amount, even 24 hour home care but funding for this is severely restricted and subject to a rigorous assessment. This means that, for practical purposes, unless you have just come out of hospital, you are almost certainly going to have to pay for extra help yourself. No matter how slender your financial resources, this is probably what you ought to be spending your money on. You have been saving money for 'a rainy day'? Well, now is the rainy day. Your anxiety about the degree to which having a stranger in the house will feel like a dreadful intrusion may be justified. But a number of our friends found that the extra time made available because, for example, of having to do fewer domestic chores, meant that they had more time for each other.

How to find help once you have decided you need it may be a tricky matter. The best route is via personal recommendations from relatives, friends or neighbours. Of course, you should note any hesitations in the way a recommendation is made and probe to find out why any ambiguity exists but if you can persuade yourself of the genuineness of the recommendation, then go for it! When you interview someone, remember you are being interviewed yourself, so give an honest account of what you need and make sure you are offering the going market rate. Unfortunately for you, you are likely to be in a seller's market.

If you fail to find someone by personal recommendation, then probably using an agency is a better idea than advertising. The advantage of an agency is that it will ensure you are always covered when your regular help is ill or on holiday. The disadvantage is that it is more expensive. Again, agencies are best found by personal recommendation. The most important attribute of carers is that they are likeable - you like them and they like you. You will never find a carer or cleaner who has exactly the same level of obsessionality as you. They all have higher or lower standards than you do. You should try and tolerate that. But having someone in the house you can't stand is never going to work out, so, if that is the case, you need to say a gracious goodbye and start looking again.

Home or residential care?

Only one of our close friends who died went into residential care during their terminal illnesses. About half died in hospital or a hospice after a relatively brief stay of a few days or at most two or three weeks. This was not a question of expense. The cost of twenty-four-hour care at home is very similar to the cost of full-time residential care. The lack of use of residential care reflects the almost universal preference for terminally ill people to stay at home for as long as possible. This preference was shared by their carers. All the same, though this rarely happened with our friends, there is sometimes an imperative need for residential care. People who live alone and who are not capable of looking after themselves, most commonly because they are suffering from dementia, will virtually always need residential care. That is why 80-90% of residents of residential care and nursing homes show some degree of dementia. As the experience of our friends illustrates (see Chapter 7) even those with quite advanced dementia can be looked after at home. What sometimes makes this impossible is the development of behaviour problems that are difficult to manage in a home context. Repeated wandering off out of the house and unprovoked aggressive behaviour are the most common problems that make this necessary.

If, for some reason, it does become necessary to consider residential care, then clearly the choice of a suitable home requires great care. Again, personal recommendation is the best source of advice. When visiting a home, the communication of kindness and respect for the residents and their relatives is probably the number one priority. Other important considerations are the quality of the rooms, the accessibility of staff, the ratio of staff to residents (including at night), the quality of the food served up and the availability to residents of stimulating occupation. Sometimes, it has to be said, visiting a number of possible homes is enough to persuade the terminally ill person and their relatives that further attention should be given to the possibility of care at home.

'Dying Tidily'

This is the name given to a folder prepared by a friend who wished to make sure that all the information that might be needed by her survivors was readily at hand in the event of her unexpected death. It is a very appropriate name for a folder prepared by a terminally ill person for the same reason. Most of us have tried to live tidily, though hopefully not too tidily, so it makes good sense to depart in similar mode. Such a folder should surely contain one's will, advance directive, registered power of attorney, passwords for computer, mobile phone and any other devices, bank account details and other relevant information.

At the same time, one should give careful attention to the need to remove stuff on one's computer one does not wish one's survivors to see. Perhaps the most appalling example of the consequences of failing to do this was demonstrated in David Baddiel's successful one man show *My Family: Not the Sitcom*. The first half of this entertainment, which must surely rank as one of the worst taste performances ever staged, was an account of the undeleted, highly explicit messages sent by David Baddiel's deceased mother to her lover over a period of some years. One of these contained the immortal line 'My clitoris is on fire for you.', a line which, Baddiel did not fail to observe, turned out to have some literal truth when her body was cremated after her death. Admittedly, few of us will have a comedian as a surviving son, let alone one with the gall to use such material in this manner, but we should all surely be careful not to take similar risks that might result in serious embarrassment to our family members.

More generally, we should try to ensure that the surviving members of our families are not left with correspondence or other papers about whose disposal they will need to make difficult decisions. This is your correspondence, and these are your papers, it is you who needs to make these decisions. Unless you are famous and someone is going to be writing your biography, they will have little interest in those you leave behind. Having said all that, most people find it extraordinarily difficult to throw away their papers and letters they have received even many years ago. Some papers may contain confidential material and you will need to make arrangements for these to be destroyed at some local waste disposal unit. If there are two of you engaged in throwing away, it is likely that one of you will be more ruthless in deciding what really needs keeping than the other. It is the ruthless one whose voice needs to prevail. If there is only one of you, then it's a good idea to bring in someone else, perhaps an adult child, another member of the family or a friend to provide an independent, ruthless voice.

Photographs are another matter. Print images can be put in albums which take up little space and much fun can be had in trying to remember where they were taken. In general, any print images of scenery or buildings can safely be destroyed but photographs of people will, in contrast to letters and papers be appreciated by later generations. They take up little space in albums. You will need to label photos so that the people in them can be identified. Digital images take up no space and those who follow you will probably have little difficulty in deciding which to delete. Of course, if you think there might be embarrassing images, either print or digital, in your albums or on your phone, you will need to make sure they are deleted.

Sizing down

For most people, the size of the house or flat in which they spend their last months or years will be adequate for their needs but no more than that. For some, however, when their children have finally left home (and this may be a protracted process), they find themselves in a place clearly too big for their needs. The question then arises whether to move to a smaller place. There are several good reasons for moving from a place that is too big for you. The costs of running and maintaining a large building may be significant. Larger places are more of a hassle to keep clean than smaller ones. If you sell your existing house for more than you buy a new establishment, you may be able to give money to your children and, if you do this seven or more years before you die, such gifts will be free of inheritance tax (see above). You may feel altruistically, you have no right to take up more space than you need when there is such a shortage of housing in the country.

There are also many good reasons for not sizing down, some practical, some financial but, above all, emotional. Giving over to strangers, during one's lifetime, a place which has so many memories is inevitably distressing perhaps not just to you but to your children, if you have any. The whole process of moving, finding a place, buying and selling, moving furniture around, making endless decisions about what to keep and what to throw, is seriously exhausting. Whether you can manage it is more a matter of fitness than age, but unless you are energetic and healthy you should not contemplate moving. Finally, moving is expensive. The costs of the estate agent, removal expenses, property tax and stamp duty are not inconsiderable. You need to take all these into account when assessing whether a move is financially sensible. If an important reason for moving is that you cannot afford the expenses of your existing house, this problem may be resolved by taking out equity release on your property. This involves obtaining a lump sum or a steady stream of income by reducing the value of your property. If you are contemplating this possibility, it is important to ensure that, if you happen to live much longer than might be expected, a point does not arise when you can be made homeless by the equity release company. If you are thinking of taking out equity release you almost certainly need good independent financial advice provided in a form you can understand. If you do equity release, you need to check with a finance adviser that funds can be accessed if you lose capacity.

Basically, there are two conditions that have to be met before you should think of sizing down. First, there have to be good reasons for wanting to move (see above) and second, there has to be some house or flat that you can afford to buy or rent where you would really like to live. Two words of warning about where to move. In general, it is not a good idea to move away to somewhere which will mean you lose contact with friends and family or will find contact with them difficult. There may be a lovely sea or lake view, but, after a few days, this probably won't compensate for the loss of your social life. It is also not a great idea to move somewhere you don't particularly like just so that you can be near a child. Your adult children are likely to be mobile and, if they move away, you may be left somewhere you would prefer not to be.

The place you move to needs to be suitable not just for your needs now but as they will be in some years' time. Will you still be able to walk up that hill to the local shops? Will the stairs be too much for you? Stairs present a particular dilemma. On the one hand, having to climb one or two flights of stairs several times a day will keep you fit and increase your expectation of life. On the other hand, if, at some point you can no longer manage the stairs, you may be marooned on the ground floor. If you have a wet room or shower and toilet on the ground floor that will not be a problem. Ideally therefore, you will either move to a flat on the ground floor or with a lift, or you will move to a house that is readily adaptable to ground floor living. An alternative is a move to sheltered accommodation. If you are in frail health and the economics are right, this is a possibility that should be seriously considered. It will relieve anxiety to know that care is available when you need it and this may compensate for the fact that your social life is likely to be limited to other elderly people.

Immediately after death

There are a number of legal formalities that must be undertaken immediately after death. First, a doctor must sign a death certificate giving the cause of death. So a family member needs to contact the general practice as soon as possible after death, and ask if a doctor can come round to sign a medical certificate. The doctor will also provide a formal notice explaining that the death must be registered and where this can be done. If the patient has not been seen by a doctor in the fourteen days before death, the death must be reported to the coroner who, in the unusual situation that there is uncertainty about the cause of death, may order a post-mortem examination. Organ donation, if this has been requested, is only possible if the organs are removed within half an hour, so, apart from the cornea which is viable for up to twenty-four hours, this will only be possible if the patient has died in hospital.

A firm of undertakers then needs to be contacted. If you do not know of one, the hospital or the family doctor will advise. There is no rush for the body to be removed, so if family members wish to stay with the body for some time, they can delay the point at which the undertaker's staff remove the body to keep until the time of the funeral.

Your funeral

Religious funerals are, at least in theory, statements about the belief system of the dead person and their family members. For example, at Church of England funerals, the minister begins the service with this quotation from the gospel of St. John, 11, 25, 26: 'I am the resurrection and the life, saith the Lord: he that believeth in me, though he were dead, yet shall he live: and whosoever liveth and believeth in me shall never die.' This implies a belief in an afterlife and indeed, an eternal life. Even from the very small sample of practising members of the Church of England among my friends, it is clear that many Christians do not believe in an afterlife, though they have a strong wish to have an Anglican funeral. The connection between the statements made in the funeral service and the belief system of the dead person and his family are tenuous.

For perhaps the majority of the population who have neither strong religious beliefs nor a clear commitment to atheism, a religious funeral is a default choice, made in the absence of an acceptable alternative. For such people, although the statements made in the funeral service by the minister do not represent, as they do for those with strong religious beliefs, a statement of the beliefs of the dead person and their family members, the funeral nevertheless performs other important functions. It is an event that symbolises the end of a life and provides a framework for disposal of the body either by burial or by cremation. It brings friends and family together to share their feelings of loss and sadness. It may be, and the stated wishes of the dead person make this clear, an excuse for a party at which stories can be told about the dead person, sometimes with tears, sometimes with laughter.

The great majority of my friends and their family members who were atheists chose not to have religious funerals, though a minority of my Jewish friends did have Jewish funerals and a small number of others asked if the Jewish mourner's prayer, the Kaddish, could be said in Hebrew at their funerals. Two Anglican friends had church funerals and one Catholic friend a funeral mass. No non-Jewish atheist friends asked to have a religious funeral. A small number of family members who survived them did however express regret at the lack of a recognised ritual to mark the end of a life.

Humanist funerals, with celebrants from Humanists UK, provide the nearest approximation to a ritual funeral, but the lack of a liturgy, the fact that the funeral is conducted not according to a widely accepted form but is individualised to match the needs of family members, means that the central features of a ritual are lacking. The nearest approximation to ritualised non-religious events is that proposed by Auguste Comte, the French positivist philosopher, who founded a 'Religion de L'humanité'. The pillars of this creed were altruism, order and progress. It had its own liturgy and priesthood. While it achieved some brief success in the late nineteenth century, it did not achieve widespread acceptance and, although there are vestiges of it which survive to this day in Brazil, it rapidly disappeared elsewhere.

The fact that, in the UK, Humanists UK, (formerly the British Humanist Association (BHA)) is the only organisation that trains celebrants to conduct non-religious funerals means that even atheists who do not have faith in science as the only source of truth (see Chapter 2) and therefore are in dispute with one of the main tenets of Humanists UK are forced to choose between asking for a Humanists UK celebrant or conducting their own funeral service. Whichever is chosen, it is possible for the main functions of such a service to be met. The event does symbolise the end of a life, it can be a statement of the belief system of the dead person and their family members, it does bring family members and friends together to share their feelings and, though it may seem inappropriate even to think this, it is an excuse for a party.

Your funeral will be the first major event in your family after your death. Even if your death is seen as a relief from suffering, your family members are likely to be in shock and not in the best frame of mind to organise this occasion. You will therefore be doing them a favour if you leave behind you some thoughts about your funeral. This may be no more than a statement that, as far as you are concerned, you really don't mind what your survivors do about a funeral; you leave it entirely up to them. At least they will then know they have carte blanche.

If, however, you do wish to leave some views as to how you want your funeral to go, it is probably better to make these known in the form of suggestions rather than instructions. After all, as a non-believer, you will not think that you are going to be present in any form at your funeral, so it is reasonable to think that those who are going to be there should have the main say in what happens. One of our late friends stated that he did not want a particular member of his family present at his funeral. This led to a great deal of embarrassment and, in the end, in my view quite rightly, this wish was ignored.

Given that proviso, it is probably better to be as specific in your suggestions as you can be. As far as music is concerned, for example, rather than 'anything by Schubert' or 'anything by Paul McCartney', it would be better to name your favourite piece. Your aim should be to reduce the need for choice when your family members are not in the best frame of mind to make choices. If you do not have any religious beliefs, you will almost certainly not wish to have a minister of any church officiate at the event, but you might make clear if you would like one of the trained celebrants of

Humanists UK, or a member of your family or a particular friend to have this responsibility.

You may well wish to give instructions as to the disposal of your body, in particular whether you wish to be buried or cremated. Some people buy a burial plot for their body or ashes before they die and at least this removes one headache as well as a financial cost from their survivors. If you are being cremated, you may well ask for your ashes to be spread in some favourite location. You might even want to suggest what is inscribed on your tombstone though unless you can rival Spike Milligan's wording 'I told you I was ill', it might be better to avoid trying to be witty.

With current concern about the environment, you may feel you wish the disposal of your body provides an opportunity to make a statement about the way death can benefit nature. Atheists, and not only atheists, are likely to think in terms of a 'green' burial. This involves, in the case of burial, the rejection of wooden coffins in favour of lightweight, biodegradable coffins which decompose into the surrounding earth. In the case of cremation, you can choose for your ashes to be stored in a biodegradable urn until such time as they are scattered in some place that is meaningful to you, your family members and your friends.

Most people have a social event to which people who attend the funeral are invited to go after the event. Again, you might wish to express some ideas where you would like this to be and what you would like to see served. Alcohol is a common suggestion. Your funeral is likely to be held when your family members and friends are still in shock. Because it is held so soon after your death, some might not even be able to get there. For this reason, an event in your memory is frequently held some weeks or months after you die. Again, you might like to express a suggestion or two about such an event. This might take the form of a formal memorial occasion or celebration or, more likely, it will just involve family and friends coming together specifically to think about you, tell stories about you, hopefully recall some of the good times they had with you. As a bonus from the HMRC, the expense of such events is tax-deductible when inheritance tax is calculated. Such an event is sometimes seen as providing 'closure' for those nearest to you. This is a misnomer for memories never close, but it may serve as providing a milestone for family members and friends in the process of preserving your place in their minds while they themselves are still alive.

CHAPTER 10

Preparing for after death

Introduction

You may have a belief in an afterlife with an extra-terrestrial or spiritual existence of some sort after death. Even, however, if you have no belief in an afterlife, you may still have a strong interest in what you leave behind. For those without religious beliefs, what we leave behind on this planet is all that is left of us. In fact, we live on after our deaths in many, many ways, to some of which we perhaps pay less regard than we should.

All our friends except one had at least one child; most had two or three with a maximum of five. By the time they died, most of my friends had grandchildren. Indeed, altogether, my twenty-four friends managed to produce an average of about four grandchildren, or about a hundred in all. Obviously, all our friends live on in the way they brought up their children, in what they transmitted to them by teaching and by example. But let me first consider their genetic inheritance.

Genes

Except for the very small number (two) of our friends' children who were born by adoption, all the children inherited half their parent's genes. Grandchildren inherit a quarter of their genes from each grandparent. While certain characteristics such as eye colour are 100% inherited, the degree of inheritance for other physical and mental characteristics varies according to the amount of variation in the society in which children grow up. In societies in which there is complete social equality, all variation in the offspring is due to genetic factors. In contrast, in societies with great inequalities, the genetic contribution to most mental and behavioural characteristics may be quite small or virtually non-existent though, of course, this is not the case for physical characteristics.

Your children and grandchildren will, because of your genetic inheritance, have some of your physical characteristics. People are bound to have commented on the way some of your children's facial features or the sound of their voices remind them of you. More complicated but also perhaps more interesting is the inheritance of personality and behaviour. The findings from scientific studies, often involving twins, of children in societies with moderately high levels of inequality such as the UK, suggest that children inherit about half their level of intelligence from their parents. Some behavioural characteristics, such as the presence of autism and attention deficit hyperactivity disorder are more highly inherited, while others, such as antisocial behaviour, depression and anxiety are much less so. These latter depend more on upbringing and experiences, although genetic influences often play some part. Certain talents, such as musical and mathematical ability appear more highly heritable than others. There were no particularly gifted musicians or mathematicians among our late friends, and this may explain why, while many inherited their parent's love of music, only two of their children became professional musicians. None became professional mathematicians though many, like their parents were highly numerate. Some characteristics are less obviously inherited though inherited they must be. For example, it is common for adult children to be mistaken for their parents when they answer the telephone and vice versa. This similarity of voice must be related both to the shape of the larynx as well as to some degree of imitation. It is impossible to know precisely to what degree our genetic inheritance has been passed on to our children; all we know is that, as a result of genetic influences, our friends passed on a sizeable number of their physical and fewer, but nevertheless a significant number of their personality and behavioural characteristics.

Social inheritance

From the time you taught your children (if you had any) how to put on their socks and shoes, to tie their shoelaces, you have been passing on skills you yourself were probably taught by your own parents. It was common for our friends to have passed on, for example, their knowledge of wild flowers, their taste in music and, if they had any as most of them did, their interest in domestic politics, to their children. The degree to which children vote the same way as their parents is striking and becomes apparent when there is a break in tradition in this respect. When voters in the broken heartlands of the industrial Midlands and north of England voted Conservative in the 2019 UK election, a common reflection of those who voted in this way was that their parents would 'turn in their graves' if they ever knew this. My own father did not waste time in transmitting his values. When, after my birth, my mother and I returned home from the maternity hospital, there was a card above my cot which contained a paraphrase of some words by Tom Paine – 'The World is Your Country, Mankind are your Brethren, To Do Good is Your Religion.'

There is some controversy whether, as Richard Dawkins, the evolutionary biologist believes, some of the characteristics acquired in life, can be embedded in your DNA and passed on to your children as part of their genetic inheritance. Dawkins coined the term 'meme' to describe these genetic components but his hypothesis has been met with considerable scepticism from others in the field. To all intents and purposes, it really doesn't matter whether your behaviour and ideas are transmitted genetically or solely by example and instruction – the effect is the same. For example, two of our late friends had sons who were gay. Both of these sons, as it happens, were also highly talented and professionally successful. The findings of scientific studies of homosexual men have left open the degree to which sexual preference is inherited. All one can say is that the sexual preferences of these men, like their high intelligence was a product of their genes and upbringing. The same has to be said for occupational choice. The only lawyers (two) among the children of our friends were born to lawyers and the only doctors (two) were children of doctors. But one of the three lawyers among our friends did not have a child who was a lawyer and of the six of our friends who were doctors, four did not have a medical child. The fact that the great majority of the children of our friends were middle-class and at least moderately successful in the careers they pursued can again be put down to a combination of genes and social transmission. Many were educated at independent schools and even among those who were state-educated, great care was taken to ensure they went to schools with a high academic reputation. It is a striking fact that only one of our late friends had been divorced and perhaps equally striking that the rate of separation and divorce was distinctly higher in their children's generation. Around half our late friends had a child who, by the time they died, had experienced a marital breakdown. The social influences on marriage breakdown of the society in which their children grew up were far more powerful than any social and genetic influences on the stability of relationships transmitted by their parents. In contrast, there is a strong similarity in religious belief between my late friends and their children. None of the children of my late friends are regular attenders at religious services, though a small number do have a religious identity and, very occasionally, a nominal affiliation to the religion of their parents. Clearly, the numbers of our late friends and their children are too small to draw any general conclusions about the nature of inheritance, but it is interesting to note that their patterns of transmission are very similar to those that have been demonstrated in large studies.

Leaving a Sense of Loss

Living through a terminal illness is, inevitably, an intense emotional experience. That experience will differ, as we saw in Chapter 6, according to circumstances. For some, death will be a relief for it will mean relief from suffering after a life well-lived. For others, it will be a sad disappointment, cutting short, for example, possibilities for seeing children or grandchildren growing up. While the dying person's emotions are taken up by such thoughts and feelings, those of close family members and friends may well be filled with quite another preoccupation, a deep sense of impending loss of the person who is dying. It may well be difficult for people whose days are numbered, to empathise with those close to them who are finding the expectation of loss extremely difficult to contemplate. Empathy with a sense of loss for oneself implies acceptance of the idea that one has value, that one's departure will mean creating a deep hole in the lives of others. Ensuring that this hole is less deep than it otherwise might be is why paying attention to practical issues, such as ensuring that one 'dies tidily' at least as far as one's financial affairs are concerned, as described in Chapter 9, is so important. Sorting out practical issues may be difficult enough, especially if one is feeling dreadfully ill, but even harder may be working out how to reduce the emotional sense of loss that will inevitably occur when one dies.

Loss, grief and bereavement of those who have lost people close to them is not a subject covered in this book which focuses instead on the experience of terminal illness. But preparatory mourning is inevitably a component of the experience of terminal illness and so needs some discussion here. It may be tempting for a terminally ill person to claim to loved ones that 'you will manage perfectly well without me' or even that 'it will be such a relief when I'm gone and you don't have to look after me and my constant moaning' but this is unlikely to be helpful. It may elicit feelings of guilt but that is probably not what you want. Instead, it is probably better to initiate a conversation by showing real interest in how things are going to be for those close to you after your departure and being prepared to listen to news and views that may not be entirely welcome. Hearing that your partner or your children expect to feel angry with you either for the way you have behaved in the past or because they see you as abandoning them is going to be difficult. But if such feelings are indeed expressed, this will give the terminally ill person the opportunity to ask for forgiveness and thus, whether or not this is forthcoming, at least it will allow the sharing of emotions between people who care for each other. It may seem bizarre to want to share the experience of the loss of oneself, but just being able to say 'It's hard for me to work out how much you are going to miss me and I'm really sorry I'm not going to be around to help you with those feelings, whatever they may be,' may be enough to provide some consolation.

In fact, a terminally ill person cannot know with any serious degree of accuracy, how people are going to think and feel about him or her after death, but they can, by influencing what is left behind in the way of stories, written memories or memoirs and photographs provide indicators how they want to be remembered.

Memories

For those without religious belief or belief in the possibility of an afterlife, memories are the main carriers of immortality. Certainly, this is the case as far as our late friends are concerned. The interview I carried out with their surviving spouse or children was not designed to recapture memories of those who had died while they were still alive. It was carried out solely for the purposes of this book and consequently focused on their terminal illnesses and their religious beliefs or lack of them. Nevertheless, despite its narrow focus, a number of my interviewees found the experience of recalling their spouses or parents a rewarding one. Some, in response to my message of thanks to them for granting me an interview, wrote back to say that they had found the process of recall a rewarding experience.

A number of our friends left published accounts of at least part of their lives. Michael Rutter and Lionel Hersov wrote about their own professional careers in articles they published in professional journals. Three of my late friends wrote a memoir. Stanley Price wrote *Somewhere to Hang Your Hat*, a hilarious account of his Irish/Jewish childhood in Dublin. He still makes me laugh, long after his death when I read his account of how he locked himself in the lavatory for several hours in a successful attempt to avoid returning to his hated boarding school. Barbara Tizard wrote a description of her early years, *Home Is Where One Starts From*. Mary Warnock, in her *Memoir: People and Places*, gives a description not only of her own life, but of several of the most interesting people she had encountered. There are many reminiscences in Jonathan Miller's collection of essays: *One Thing and Another*. Two of my friends merited a full-length biography. Kate Bassett's *Jonathan Miller: In Two Minds*, describes his life especially as an opera and theatre director. My *Mary Warnock: Ethics, Education and Public Policy in Post-War Britain* gives a full account of her life.

In addition, two of the children of our friends have published an account of their lives which includes an extended description of their parents, thus immortalising them for at least one new generation. Jonathan Miller's son has written an account of his upbringing in *Gloucester Crescent: Me, My Dad and other Grown-Ups*. This includes an extended portrait of his father, seen through the eyes of an affectionate, if, at times, wryly humorous child. Felix Warnock in his account of his career as a musician and musical administrator *Perfection Is Not The Word For It,* has described his parents, including my late friend, his mother, in some detail, though with rather little emphasis on her considerable musical ability and interests.

Jonathan Miller is also on record on Youtube giving an account of his childhood and later experiences as a director of operas, plays and television documentaries. There are published obituaries of all these as well as a number of others of our friends, published in national newspapers. I have, of course, my own rich memories of these friends as does my wife, but these will not outlive us and, given our ages, they do not have a very long shelf life. It is in the memories of their children, grandchildren and younger friends and colleagues that they will live on.

The great majority of people do not have obituaries written about them and memories of them lie solely in the minds of their friends and family members. But, at some point in their lives, many people have a strong desire to know more about the lives their parents led, and who better than you to leave a written record, a memoir or perhaps an audio account? Writing a memoir, perhaps supplemented by photographs, can be a rewarding experience but for some reason, not many people get round to it. This is usually to do with a lack of confidence about committing thoughts to paper, though sometimes it arises from a sense of shame or regret about past events. Some people mistakenly think that their lives have been too humdrum to be worth recording. For people with means, it is always possible to find writers, who, for a fee, will listen to you talking about your life and then write a book or at least an extended account of it. Indeed, there is now a small industry employing large numbers of ghost writers. But, for most people, writing a memoir is going to be up to them.

Jonathan Miller, Mary Warnock, Barbara Tizard and Stanley Price were all people who found a wide readership for their memoirs. You will probably feel more than satisfied if the surviving members of your family and your friends find your account of your own life interesting and rewarding. If, however, you do write a memoir and give it to your children, you must be prepared to be disappointed in the reception. Your children are quite likely, in my experience, to put it aside for reading at some later date. They may never read it while you are alive, but rest assured, there will come a time when they want to know more about their roots and it at this point they will thank you for having given them an invaluable resource.

So, how to go about writing a memoir? My advice is to do the easy bits first, If there was a time in your life that was particularly interesting or enjoyable, then write about that first. Once you've written a few paragraphs, hopefully, you will have gained some confidence and will want to write some more, perhaps about your own parents and your childhood. Many people claim that they have very weak recollections of their childhood, adolescence and early adult life. It is a common experience to find that, once one starts writing, perhaps stimulated by photographs and surviving letters, memories begin to surface to a surprising degree. Discussions with brothers and sisters with whom you grew up are also powerful memory stimulants. If you have difficulty getting going, you may be helped by attendance at one of the courses available both online and face to face on writing a memoir. Remember you are under no obligation to write down episodes in your life that you regret or are ashamed of. You can just write what you want. If you depart wildly from reality, then maybe you will find you have written a novel! This could be just as interesting and incidentally, as self-revealing as a memoir.

The exercise of writing a memoir can be combined with an exploration of your family history. Again, there are web sites and courses that can assist you. Taking a DNA test and putting yourself in touch with family members with whom you have lost touch or indeed, with whom you have never been in touch, can put your own life in a new context of which you had previously been unaware and will certainly be of interest to family members who survive you.

The Future Without You

You will naturally be sad to be missing the future of your family and friends, perhaps thinking you cannot be helpful if they run into trouble or be there to celebrate happy occasions. In fact, of course, you will be with them in their minds and be especially remembered at celebrations. Further, during your lifetime, you do have the possibility of a more explicit influence on their lives after your death in both a positive and a negative sense. For example, in the talks you have with your partner/husband/wife or children about their lives after your death, you might well wish to tell them you do not want them to feel in any way inhibited in what they do by thoughts about what you would or would not have wanted. Most widows and widowers will not wish to form new partnerships, but they are likely to value the thought that you would want them to be absolutely free to do whatever they might wish. Now this might well not accord with how you feel. You would not be human if you did not have envious thoughts about someone taking your place. But it is important to distinguish between possessiveness and love. Those you leave behind will want to think you loved them enough not to want thoughts of them to stand in their way whatever life decisions they make. Some people leave income to their partners until such time as they form new partnerships when the income stops. Hopefully, you will feel sufficient trust in your partner to make this unnecessary. The fewer conditions you apply to what you leave, the more certain your partner can be that they were really loved. As far as your children and grandchildren are concerned, they too will want to feel they are not constrained by thoughts of what you would have wished or not wished for them. Just let them be!

As I write in the summer of 2023, the world and perhaps particularly the UK, seems to be in a truly dreadful state. A combination of Brexit, the Covid epidemic and chronic mismanagement by its government has made my country a financial disaster area. It currently suffers from high levels of childhood poverty as well as gross income inequality with many having to choose between eating enough to survive and heating their homes to a tolerable level. The war in Ukraine is costing tens of thousands of young male lives and threatens to drive western Europe into even worse financial chaos that it is experiencing presently. Climate change will, except in the unlikely event of global cooperation, gradually burn all our forests and flood vast areas that are low-lying making them uninhabitable. What a world to pass on to one's children!

It is a small consolation that the world that was passed on to me when I was born in 1932 was also in terrible shape. Just the following year, Hitler took power and triggered a world war with greater loss of life than in any previous conflict. Yet after 1945 the world became a better place and enjoyed three quarters of a century (nearly all my adult life) of relative calm and increasing prosperity with lower and lower levels of inequality. There seems little prospect of such a tranquil time recurring in the foreseeable future. Yet, who knows? The amazing technological advances that have been made in my time at least provide the means for global collaboration on a scale that would not previously have been thought possible. There is a younger generation that has a mixture of competence and energy that might yet make the world a better place. I love to think it will.

CHAPTER 11

Going Gentle

Introduction

There are various versions of what might be called a 'gentle' death. The first is the instantaneous demise. No warning, no pain, no anxiety, just gone from one moment to the next. Now that is all very well for the person who suddenly dies but is far from ideal for those who remain. No time for preparation, no opportunity to say goodbye, just a terrible shock. If we accept, as we should, that death is a social as well as an individually experienced event, then sudden death can only be seen as far from what one might desire. But, of course, those who die more or less instantaneously have no choice in the matter.

Another version of the 'gentle' death can be described as follows. After a full and happy life, a very old individual develops symptoms which are rapidly diagnosed as terminal. Medical care, given by doctors and nurses who have known the patient well before the illness ensure that symptoms are so well controlled that only mild discomfort is experienced. After about six weeks, with plenty of opportunity for family members and friends to say their goodbyes, with their close family around them, the individual gradually becomes sleepier, goes into a coma and dies. Unfortunately, such a terminal illness may well not occur, usually because the nature of the final illness does not allow it but sometimes because there are unavoidable circumstances which get in the way. It is not that easy to stage manage a 'gentle' death.

Some descriptions of healthcare professional assisted deaths portray final hours which are as 'gentle' as can be imagined. Death occurs very rapidly at a time of the individual's choosing with close family around to share the last moments. However, the criteria for an assisted death in those countries where it has been legalised involve the experience of persistent suffering over a significant period of time before it is agreed that such a death is permissible, so this can certainly not be regarded as the most desirable form of terminal illness.

So what are the best ways one can ensure that one goes as 'gentle' as possible? Here are some suggestions, based largely but not entirely on the experiences of my late friends and their family members and on what I have read.

Preparation for death needs to begin as early as possible. Opportunities should be taken for talking about death with children. These may arise on the death of an elderly relative or a pet. Questions children ask about death should be honestly answered in as matter of fact a way as possible. Children will then come to view death not just as the end but as a part of life. Throughout life, conversations about death should neither be avoided nor obsessively pursued. They should be seen as occasions to share sadness and loss as well as celebrations for lives well lived. Then, when one's own turn comes, one will be able to face talking about it with previous experiences that help us to find the right words.

A gentle death is more likely to be possible if there is good communication with the various health professionals who may be involved in the last weeks and months. This is a time when continuity of care is especially desirable. Doctors and nurses are always short of time, and one hopes they will spend as little as possible catching up with one's details on the computer. Further, though it is difficult to understand why because it is part of their job, some doctors and nurses themselves find it difficult to talk about dying and death. In earlier chapters I have discussed how one can make it easier for them. The same holds for communication between husbands and wives, partners and friends. By being open oneself one can encourage others to be the same, but it doesn't always work that way. Some people function best on denial, and they deserve respect too.

Clearly, good symptom control is important in achieving as gentle a death as possible. Nowadays, what is written about terminal illness often emphasises the importance of avoiding over-medicalisation. It is true that some people are kept alive by insensitive doctors quite beyond a time when their lives are worth living. A gentle death is far more a medical triumph than a few more months of pointless suffering. But under-medicalisation is also to be avoided. Not giving adequate pain relief because of the danger of addiction is just silly when the patient is not going to live long enough for addiction to develop.

Gauging the right quantity and quality of support and care in the last weeks and months is often not easy. This is likely to be provided by family members, friends and paid carers. A gatekeeper, often a spouse, partner or child may be essential. Do not expect vast expressions of empathy and compassion in those providing care. Just try to make sure they are tactful and kind.

Try not to be doctrinaire about where terminal care is provided. Home is likely to be the best place if it is possible to arrange good care there. If this becomes no longer possible, then admission to a hospice if a place is available is likely to be the next best option. If this is not available then admission to hospital may be unavoidable. Admissions to both hospices and hospitals will work out better if there can be a family member present by the bedside for the waking hours right up to the moment of death. This is particularly important if the terminally ill person has dementia, but even people with good cognitive function will appreciate continuing company, even if they may prefer to be alone with their own thoughts for some of the time.

Terminally ill people with troubling thoughts that will not go away need to see a counsellor, or, if they have religious faith, a priest. There are many techniques for coping with such thoughts, including cognitive therapy and mindfulness. Probably the technique used is less important than the opportunity to share distressing preoccupations with someone who is understanding and not judgemental. Terminally ill people with religious faith know that they will soon be faced with a divine judge, whose verdict is unknowable. Those without such faith can take comfort in their awareness that there are professionals around whose job it is to be understanding rather than judgemental.

At the very end of life, 'going gentle' is likely to involve gradually increasing sleepiness before entering a coma. If this can happen with people, - family or friends present whom one loves and is loved by, all the better. If this is not possible, then one might bring such people to mind and, in one final effort of imagination, enjoy their company to the last.

Acknowledgements

I am particularly grateful to my wife, Nori, for her help with the sections on dementia, to my daughter, Anna for general medical advice and to Robert Schon for legal advice. I am also grateful to the following for the considerable assistance they gave me with the content:

Eleanor Ames

Nick Barlay

Robert Cassen

Maggie Cohen

Edmund Fawcett

Julian Hughes

Jeanne Katz

Frances Pinter

Stephen Reicher

John Tusa

Sarah Wootton

Sue Ziebland

I am also most grateful to the family members of my late friends who allowed me to interview them and to quote from their interviews.

I should like to thank Faber and Faber for permission to quote lines from Philip Larkin's *Aubade* and David Higham Associates for permission to include the quotation by Herbert Read.

Any errors are entirely my responsibility.

Further reading

Julian Barnes (2009) Nothing To Be Frightened Of. London, Vintage Books

Ann Cartwright and Clive Seale (1990) The Natural History of a Survey. King Edward's Hospital for London.

Andrew Copson and Alice Roberts (2023) The Little Book of Humanist Funerals, London, Piatkus

Atul Gawande (2015) Being Mortal. Profile Books

John Gray (2018) Seven Types of Atheism, London, Penguin Books

Sam Harris (2014) Waking Up: Searching for Spirituality Without Religion. London, Penguin

David Jarrett (2020) 33 Meditations on Death, Black Swan

Shelly Kagan (2012) Death. Yale University Press

Robert Keats (2017) How To Die Well Without God. Robert Keats

Kathryn Mannix (2017) With the End in Mind. Penguin

Sean O'Mahony (2016) The Way We Die Now. Head of Zeus

Lucy Pollock (2021) The Book About Getting Older. Penguin Press

James Warner and Nori Graham (2018) *A Pocket Guide to Understanding Alzheimer's Disease and Other Dementias*. London, Jessica Kingsley.

Sarah Wootton and Lloyd Riley (2020) Last Rights: The Case for Assisted Dying. London, Biteback Publishing

Memoirs by my late friends

Michael Rutter (1983) A Measure of our Values, London, Quaker Home Press

Barbara Tizard (2010) Home is Where One Starts From: One Woman's Memoir, London, Word Power Books

Jonathan Miller One Thing and Another: (2018) Collected Writing 1954-2016, London, Bloomsbury Press

Stanley Price (2003) Somewhere to Hang my Hat: An Anglo-Jewish Journey, New Island Books

Biographies of my late friends

Kate Bassett: In Two Minds: A Biography of Jonathan Miller

Philip Graham: (2021) Mary Warnock: Ethics, Education and Public Policy in Post-War Britain, Cambridge, Open Books Publishers

Useful web sites

https://www.secularism.org.uk/

https://healthtalk.org/https://healthtalk.org/

https://www.cochranelibrary.com/

https://www.gov.uk/benefits-end-of-life

https://compassionindying.org.uk/

https://www.dignityindying.org.uk/

https://www.nhs.uk/conditions/social-care-and-support-guide/care-services-equipment-and-care-homes/care-homes/

https://www.hospiceuk.org/

https://www.alzheimers.org.uk/

http://www.dignitas.ch/?lang=en

https://www.gov.uk/make-will/writing-your-will

https://humanists.uk/ceremonies/non-religious-funerals/

Index